Truth is the Best Propaganda:
Edward R. Murrow's Speeches in the Kennedy Years

Nancy Snow, Ph.D.

Library of Congress Cataloging-in-Publication Data

Snow, Nancy, Truth is the Best Propaganda: Edward R. Murrow's Speeches in the Kennedy Years, U.S. History, Edward R. Murrow, international relations, 20th century geopolitics

Summary: After years as a pioneering journalist, Edward R. Murrow became the chief diplomat of the U.S. as John F. Kennedy's appointment to the Voice of America. This is a collection of his speeches with commentary and analysis.

ISBN: 978-1-939282-24-8

Published by Miniver Press, LLC, McLean Virginia
Copyright 2013 Nancy Snow

All rights reserved under International and Pan-American Copyright Conventions. By payment of the required fees, you have been granted the non-exclusive, non-transferable right to access and read the text of this e-book on-screen. No part of this text may be reproduced, transmitted, down-loaded, decompiled, reverse engineered, or stored in or introduced into any information storage and retrieval system, in any form or by any means, whether electronic or mechanical, now known or hereinafter invented, without the express written permission of Nell Minow. For information regarding permission, write to editor@miniverpress.com

First edition November 2013

Table of Contents

Introduction I
Chapter 1 Edward R. Murrow at USIA: A Personal Journey 1
Chapter 2 Brand Murrow 11
Chapter 3 The Murrow Narrative 23
Chapter 4 The Ideas Challenger 31
Chapter 5 Mania for Murrow 37
Chapter 6 Murrow, Kennedy, and Controversy 45
Chapter 7 Murrow Fails an Integrity Test 59
Chapter 8 The Murrow Doctrine in Public Diplomacy 67
Part Two The Speeches of Edward R. Murrow 73
   1. Congressional Statement, March 14, 1961 75
   2. National Press Club, May 24, 1961 83
   3. Radio Television News Directors Association, September 30, 1961 .. 109
   4. Forum Dinner with Hollywood, November 5, 1961 121
   5. The Lincoln Group of D.C., February 10, 1962 143
   6. American Management Association, February 16, 1962 155
   7. National Association of Broadcasters, March 2, 1962 167
   8. American Advertising Federation, June 19, 1963 177
   9. National Education Association, July 1, 1963 191
   10. Federal Bar Association, September 26, 1963 199
End Notes 215

Introduction

This book is a selection of, and commentary on, Edward R. Murrow's speeches as director of the United States Information Agency. Although I am a scholar, in this case, the book is not so much a scholarly project as a labor of love. In the early to mid-1990s I worked at an obscure government foreign affairs agency called the United States Information Agency, known in Washington as USIA and overseas as the U.S. Information Service or USIS. I was a newly minted Ph.D. from the School of International Service at American University in Washington, D.C., where I had been living since returning from my Fulbright year in the Federal Republic of Germany. Not wanting to be known as a Ph.D. without practical work experience, I applied for a Presidential Management Fellowship, a two-year program that provides leadership and training in the planning and management of public programs in the Federal Service. One of the open slots was at USIA, which I must admit was a complete unknown to me at the time, but at least it kept me in Washington. My first book, *Propaganda, Inc.*, now in its third edition, is a critical assessment of my experience working at the Agency in the 1990s during the first few years of the Clinton administration.

Edward R. Murrow is America's most famous and highly regarded journalist of the last century. He died nearly a half century ago, but we still hear his name in reference to the best that journalism ever was and could be. After Murrow left CBS, President John F. Kennedy nominated him to head USIA, an appointment he held through ill health for three years (January 1961 - January 1964). When I began to think about how I might commemorate this appointment, I focused on that famous phrase that Murrow shared before a U.S. House of Representatives Committee on Foreign Affairs on March 28, 1963: truth is the best propaganda. It stands out for its obvious contradiction. Propaganda is conventionally associated with the shading of truth, not revealing all facts, but just the facts that work in favor of the sponsor of those facts. Murrow wasn't speaking in absolutes. He didn't say, for instance, **the** truth is the best propaganda. He was speaking in the context of the age, an ideological struggle for power and influence between the USSR and the USA.

It was the early 1960s and Murrow was working for an administration overwhelmed by a formidable foe, the Soviet Communist regime and its global efforts to shape other countries in its Marxist-Leninist ideologies. Murrow's task through his more than 12,000 employees was to "report events in context…. We do not lie, we do not cheat, we do not suppress—and as a result, we are able to obtain a high degree of believability and persuasiveness. It is this believability and persuasiveness that so enrages the communists."[1]

Having worked firsthand for a government propaganda agency, I know that we never present the unvarnished truth, but the packaging of information in alignment with official U.S. policy and national interests. It's a compromise for the sake of policy. Here is how Murrow explained the narrative to the committee:

> Everywhere we seek to encourage constructive public support for what the President has described as 'a peaceful world community of free and independent states, free to choose their own future and their own system so long as it does not threaten the freedom of others.' We present the United States as a strong, democratic, dynamic nation qualified to lead world efforts toward this goal. We emphasize the ways in which U.S. policies harmonize with those of other peoples and governments, and underline those aspects of American life and culture which facilitate sympathetic understanding of our policies. We endeavor to unmask and counter hostile attempts on the part of communists and others to distort or frustrate American objectives and policies.

This is the open-sourced version of what USIA was doing. It parallels Kennedy's remarks that immediately follow his most famous passage in his inaugural address: "My fellow citizens of the world: ask not what America will do for you, but what together we can do for the freedom of man."

There was also another, covert directive oriented toward countering Soviet influence in the developing world, such as the Congo, Laos, Vietnam, and of course, Cuba. John F. Kennedy was a student of political theory and one doctrine he was especially fond of was counterinsurgency, which referred to efforts to counter Soviet-inspired guerrilla warriors through both military and psychological means. Kennedy came to power when many new nations were being formed through decolonization. Soviet Premier Khrushchev had openly challenged the United States in general and the Kennedy administration specifically when he said that the Soviets would guide and assist these new nations in their liberation from imperial capitalists. A Congressional hearing was held to analyze Khrushchev's speech in January 1961,[2] just a month after Kennedy sent 400 Green Beret special advisers to South Vietnam to conduct trainings in counterinsurgency against the Viet Cong.

The Soviet direct intervention in the Third World was antithetical to U.S. political and economic interests, which is why Kennedy's inaugural address had so much global focus: "Let every nation know, whether it wishes us well or ill, that we shall pay any price, bear any burden, meet any hardship, support any friend, oppose any foe, to insure the survival and the success of liberty." The U.S. government response, with its narrative of modernization and democratic nation-building, is reflected in the selection of Edward R. Murrow's USIA speeches that follow, a narrative crafted in response to the top-down Soviet communism paradigm that enforced a lowest-common denominator equality among its citizens.

Murrow needed to address the Soviet critique of the "self-serving imperial capitalists" who exploited workers and failed to achieve racial equality, but since these USIA speeches are for various American audiences, they only go so far with self-criticism. Some speeches, such as the ones Murrow gave before Hollywood, the National Association of Broadcasters, and the Radio Television News Directors Association, do a solid job of showing his efforts at reminding private industry of its responsibilities to the official American narrative.

However, his American audiences mostly wanted to see a famous Kennedy appointee and hear him talk about how well spent their taxes were on telling America's great story to the world.

Murrow's USIA was tapped to play its part in the psychological and opinion-shaping branch of counterinsurgency, a 1960s version of what we would call today the "winning hearts and minds" campaigns that were made so public after 9/11 in Afghanistan and Iraq specifically and the War on Terror in general. Unlike Eisenhower's culture-driven USIA, Kennedy and Murrow shared the attitude that USIA was a policy body and a cultural agency. Murrow's contribution to policy was not to make it so much as be aware of it so that he could be "in on the takeoffs, and not just the crash landings."[3] Murrow biographer Alexander Kendrick said "the Bay of Pigs brought Murrow into the Administration with both feet."[4] After the Bay of Pigs, Murrow became a member of a Special Group on Counterinsurgency that included the president's brother Robert F. Kennedy and principals from the Agency for International Development (AID), State Department, CIA, Joint Chiefs of Staff, and Secretary of Defense; and staff from these offices participated in counterinsurgency training programs.

Whereas historical record exalts the journalistic record of Murrow from the 1930s through 1950s, it leaves us mostly hanging in Murrow's propaganda heritage of the 1960s. This book is a contribution to the record of Murrow as chief public diplomat. We need to understand what he had to say during his tenure as USIA director so that a more complete picture of the man emerges. He was not just America's most famous journalist, but he is arguably one of its premier psychological warriors.

This book is not so much about the covert Murrow whose agency became intertwined with military intelligence activities but more about the public Murrow who headed USIA. It offers insight into the public relations activities of this popular director, what he told the layperson, industry person, or Hollywood director about the work of a government propaganda agency of the U.S. government. There are efforts to bring the covert USIA out in the open, such as the digital archive exhibit on the life and work of Edward R. Murrow at USIA at Tufts University by Dr. Susanne Belovari[5] and research by Robert J. Kodosky on USIA's Joint United States Public Affairs Office in Vietnam.[6] I applaud this research, but this book is focused solely on open-sourced propaganda efforts or above-board international relations.[7] I have never worked in covert propaganda efforts but I did have some experience with open propaganda programs designed for overseas audience consumption, including speakers, film programs, and student exchanges, and it is this fourth dimension of foreign affairs—public diplomacy—that this book involves.[8] As a public scholar, I'm most interested in offering something new to readers who may not know much about Murrow's background and time at the U.S. Information Agency.

There is no question that this journey has changed me more than any other research enterprise. I received initial support for this book from the Arthur W. Page Center at Penn State University. As a Page Legacy scholar, I proposed a book that would examine the intersection and juxtaposition between journalism and advocacy communication through the USIA speeches of Edward R. Murrow, the man who wore those two persuasive hats. I have had the joy of listening to Murrow speak the words of so many of these USIA speeches, thanks to the help of archivist Laurie Austin at the John F. Kennedy Presidential Library and Museum at Columbia Point in Boston, who very conveniently transcribed Murrow's speeches on CDs for eventual downloading on my iPod. Now I can actually go on walks with Murrow by my side. Laurie and the entire staff at this most gorgeous living museum to Kennedy's legacy were gracious and generous in their support of this research project. Through active listening of these long-ago words, I have come to the realization that while in foreign policy and public affairs actions always speak louder than words—Murrow said so repeatedly in these speeches—words still matter, what we say and how we say them. That's why I agree with my friend and public diplomacy colleague Nick Cull who says that listening is the most important dimension of public diplomacy.[9] You must listen to understand. I've always emphasized in my writings and talks that the two to one ratio between ears and mouth is for a very good reason. We just sometimes forget that ratio.

As with all my writings, this book is first and foremost for my students. It is not a comprehensive collection, but rather a select sample of what Murrow said he was doing at USIA for an audience that was not his constituency directly, but indirectly though funding. It is important to look back at what Murrow was saying fifty years ago because he has lessons for Washington today, which I spell out in more detail in my essays that preface each speech.

Edward R. Murrow was a great storyteller because he was an American craftsman of words. In the beginning were his words, the voice that spoke these words, and to the end, the words he left us. Words are all we have of him now, but they have much to teach us, if we just listen.

It is my hope that this book, which includes a selection of Murrow's most memorable speeches from 1961 to 1963, will make a contribution toward searing our memories with Edward R. Murrow's place in American public diplomacy history as his omnipresent cigarette sears practically every photograph of him on record.

With John F. Kennedy

Chapter 1

Edward R. Murrow at USIA: A Personal Journey

American traditions and the American ethic require us to be truthful, but the most important reason is that truth is the best propaganda and lies are the worst. To be persuasive we must be believable; to be believable we must be credible; to be credible we must be truthful. It is as simple as that.
　　Edward R. Murrow, 1963

Washington is the seat of American, if not global, power, which as we know from our study of Henry Kissinger is the ultimate aphrodisiac. Former presidential candidate Mo Udall said one could never fully leave Washington because of the disease called Potomac Fever, whose only cure was embalming fluid. I have managed to break away from Washington over the last several decades but that fever has remained low-grade and ever a presence in my teachings and writings. I'm proud to say that I've been able to "convert" a few students to having an interest, if not a love, of all things political. Many are naturally turned off by politics, but I try to get them to view the subject as fundamentally about two things that generally interest them: relationships (power) and money (resources). Most of them want more of both, so that's how I try to hook them. One student exclaimed with a smile that she was forever sorry for having taken one of my classes because I had her reading the newspaper and following the goings on in Washington. Sigh.

I was terribly excited to be working in foreign affairs at the United States Information Agency, actually getting my hands "dirty" as opposed to just learning about foreign affairs in a book or graduate seminar. Truthfully, USIA was responsible not so much for the making of foreign policy as it was for the placing of it in the most helpful context; for the making we had our richer, more visible cousins at the U.S. Department of State. USIA in the 1990s was still responsible for something I thought equally important: "Telling America's Story to the World," a phrase I saw every day as I walked into our building at 301 C Street, Northwest, just off the venerable Mall in Washington and blocks away from my favorite museum, Air and Space. (USIA's original location was on Pennsylvania Avenue near the White House.) We ran a multimedia operation that told America's story through person-to-person interaction, books, films, artists, exhibits, and international broadcasting. Everything we did was for overseas consumption, not for domestic distribution, so I never could make my friends and family quite understand what I was doing. I assured them that I was working at U-S-I-A, not C-I-A, because if I were at the latter I likely could neither confirm nor deny.

The 1990s were heady times, or so it seemed. The Cold War was still a lingering presence, as new and unpredictable as its end had been, and we were reading essays by Francis Fukuyama ("The End of History") and Samuel Huntington ("The Clash of Civilizations") to try to make sense of our "new world order," a phrase mostly credited to the last Cold War president, George H.W. Bush, who had just been beaten by the youthful Southern politician, Bill Clinton. The Clinton era had no real jazzy title other than the post-Cold War era, which was a thundering ugh to work with. Much less generic was my big boss, William Jefferson Clinton. I was now working for President Clinton, or at least this was how it was explained to me at USIA. As an independent foreign affairs agency, we answered to the White House. I was even asked to prepare talking points about valuing educational and cultural exchange for Clinton's first inaugural address in January 1993. The Agency veterans at the time were very excited to have a Rhodes scholar in the White House and my doctoral dissertation on "Fulbright Scholars as Cultural Mediators" offered evidence that sponsored government exchanges helped to forge closer economic and intercultural ties. To have an inaugural reference made to these exchanges, a pillar of public diplomacy, would have been a coming out party for the agency, since we were not a well-known government entity. Though my remarks weren't included in Clinton's speech, I was tapped to do publicity for the Bureau for Educational and Cultural Affairs and in that capacity I participated in some academic forums, wrote news articles, and provided remarks for some agency higher-ups. It helped that I held a doctorate and could hold my own with other academics since I wasn't yet a full-time faculty member at a university.

Throughout my two years working at USIA, I gradually began to appreciate the history and role of the Agency and the influence that its most famous director, Edward R. Murrow, had on its rhetorical significance. I still hold dear to my original assessment in *Propaganda, Inc.* that the role of a cultural affairs and international communication agency should stand on its own terms and not be commingled with American business interests overseas. Just as Murrow illustrates in his USIA speeches, I value storytelling, whether foreign or domestic, as an exercise in human engagement and find it difficult to put a dollar amount on it other than "priceless." Under Clinton, we were asked to relate what we were doing to America's economic engagement with the world. This included linking USIA programs to NAFTA (the North American Free Trade Agreement), and measuring the economic impact of artist exchanges. All of this left me very uninspired at times and lacking enthusiasm for our greater cause. Whenever I needed a reprieve, I would go downstairs to the basement of the building and visit the USIA Library. It was here that I began to note the history of the Agency, including its directors. One of those directors, arguably the director of the Agency, was Edward R. Murrow.

Until I began working on this labor of love I did not grasp that I worked for USIA exactly thirty years after Murrow. He was a Kennedy political appointee, the most famous appointee of the administration given his many years moderating popular programs like "See It Now" and "Person to Person." During his three-year tenure in Washington from January 1961 to January 1964, Murrow often identified himself as a journalist turned propagandist. I was employed as an American propagandist at the same agency for two years from October 1992 to October 1994. When Murrow left his Washington employ, he returned to his farm in upstate New York and died a year and three months later. I left Washington and began a career as a professor. Two decades later, I still can't shake that USIA motto, "Telling America's Story to the World," as it has become the backdrop mantra to almost every speech or major publication in my academic career. This book is no different.

What I have concluded from researching his twenty-five career as a professional communicator and analyzing speeches by Murrow as director of the United States Information Agency, is this: Murrow is perhaps the greatest American storyteller in both an official and unofficial capacity of the last century. Certainly no other person can match Murrow's ability to dominate across a variety of media platforms in radio, television, print, and oral communication. Eric Sevareid, one of "Murrow's Boys" at CBS, said of Murrow at the time of his death, "He was a shooting star and we will live in his afterglow a very long time." Today we need much more than his afterglow. We have never matched his kind, nor will we ever see his kind again, and I'm referring as much to American journalism as I am to American public diplomacy.

In my coming-home journey to USIA, I reached out to several people who were connected to Murrow during his Kennedy years. The preeminent historian David McCullough (Truman, John Adams), then in his late twenties, served as editor of an Arab language magazine, and described the good fortune associated with working at USIA during the Kennedy years:

> When John F. Kennedy came along and asked us to do something for our country, I took it to heart, quit Time-Life and went to Washington to look for a job in government where I could be of service. I wound up working at the United States Information Agency (USIA) for three years, which, in many ways, was the best thing that could have happened to me. I was thrown into a job that was way over my head. It was truly a "sink or swim" situation. I was put in charge of a magazine that the USIA published for the Arab world, and I knew absolutely nothing about the Arab world. I told this to the fellow who had hired me, and all he said was, "You're going to learn a lot then."[10]

David McCullough, Jr. said that his father remembers Murrow's USIA "both fondly and well."[11]

John P. Cosgrove, president of the National Press Club in Washington during the Kennedy years, introduced Murrow at his first public address after becoming USIA director. As I was listening to the audio of Murrow's NPC speech, I so enjoyed the repartee between Murrow and Cosgrove that I thought it would have been nice to meet that funny Mr. Cosgrove. On a whim I Googled Cosgrove's name and came across a recent article announcing his donation of a thousand books, personal papers, and documents of his six-decade journalism career to his hometown public library, the Pittston Memorial Library in Pittston, Pennsylvania, which he followed up with a cash donation of $50,000.[12] Within minutes I was on the phone to Washington with this nonagenarian whose claim to fame, among many others, is having met every president since Herbert Hoover.

George Stevens, Jr., who became head of the Motion Pictures Division at USIA under Murrow told me this about working with Murrow at USIA: "It was, indeed, an exciting period—and contrary to what has been written in some accounts, Murrow loved the job and the challenge. He was a superb leader of USIA and had everyone playing over their heads."[13] Several Agency employees from the Murrow days like Stanley Silverman, former budget director, and Public Affairs Officer Fred Coffey, told me about shaking the "genuine" grip of Murrow at USIA headquarters.[14] There were far too many who had already passed on, including Tom Sorensen (d. 1997), Murrow's deputy in policy and plans, and the author of the definitive work on American propaganda, *The Word War*, that includes several outstanding chapters on Murrow's tenure in Washington. Donald M. Wilson, who was part of the troika along with Murrow and Sorensen, served as Murrow's deputy. In the course of my research I came across Don's self-published *The First 78 Years*,[15] which gives the definitive personal account of what it was like serving with Ed Murrow at USIA. Wilson's wife Susan promised that she would let Don, who was battling dementia, know about my project.

I also would have loved to know Senator J. William Fulbright's (d. 1995) perspective on Murrow. They were born just three years apart in the first decade of the 20th century. Both were men of the South, though Murrow would move as a young boy of six to the Pacific Northwest. Fulbright was as prominent an elected official in Washington as Murrow was prominent as a journalist. Both were intellectual and dissenting types who believed in questioning the status quo. Both were internationalists who loved analyzing America's place in the world. Each has left an indelible mark in international education, with Murrow's first professional paid job as assistant director of the Institute of International Education, and Fulbright's sponsorship of the Fulbright educational exchange program, managed in part by the Institute of International Education. Fulbright, who was born in 1905, outlived Murrow by three decades, which gave him time to write several well-regarded political books. My 2006 book, *The Arrogance of American Power*, a critical account of the George W. Bush administration's foreign policy, is a nod to Fulbright's 1966 book, *The Arrogance of Power*. Fulbright's book criticized American intervention in Vietnam and the Johnson administration's domino theory justification that such intervention was necessary since it had Cold War politics dimensions. (Reagan would use a similar domino theory justification in the 1980s for aiding the Contras in Nicaragua.)

I knew J. William Fulbright during my graduate school years living in Washington, as well as his wife, Harriet Mayer Fulbright, whom I still know and who has done great work with the J. William and Harriet Fulbright Center. In 1992, shortly after Bill Clinton's first term presidential election, I interviewed the Arkansas senator about his Little Rock protégé for my friend Patricia Keegan's magazine, *Washington International*. Pat and I went to Fulbright's downtown office in Washington and Fulbright said with a wink, "What kept you? You came just in time. I am just about to expire."[16] When Pat told that to Harriet Fulbright a few years ago she gave a hearty laugh and said, "That was typical of him. He had a great sense of humor." I should have connected the dots back then. Fulbright was the chairman of the Senate Foreign Relations Committee that oversaw Murrow's congressional confirmation as the director of the United States Information Agency on March 14, 1961. At the conclusion of his confirmation hearing at which Murrow repeated his emphasis that the Agency would operate on the "basis of truth," Murrow had this exchange with Chairman Fulbright:

> The Chairman: Well, Mr. Murrow, we appreciate your coming here. I only have one comment. We all are agreed about telling the truth. The only trouble I find is the difficulty in finding out what the truth is, both here and abroad. I very rarely recognize what I read in the paper as having any relationship to what goes on in the Congress. There is, it seems to me, a tendency that I think is inherent in our competitive system, to emphasize the bizarre, the exotic, and the unusual. Lost in the shuffle is any sober and straightforward statement which does not build circulation or does not have appeal for some reason or other. I find it very difficult to find out what the truth is. Haven't you found that?
>
> Murrow: Yes, sir.
>
> The Chairman: It is very easy to say we are going to spread the truth, but I predict you will have a very difficult time finding out what the truth is.

It was at J. William Fulbright's funeral on February 17, 1995, at the National Cathedral in Washington that I finally met Fulbright's protégé, President Bill Clinton. I'm known as one who is never at a loss for words, but at that meeting I was.

At the time of this publication, it's the 50th anniversary year of John F. Kennedy's assassination in Dallas on November 22, 1963. A little over two decades after Kennedy's death, I was a Fulbright exchange student to the Federal Republic of Germany. I walked into the home of my host family and saw a picture of Kennedy displayed prominently on the wall of their living home. To this working-class German host family, to the world and to many Americans, Kennedy remains the face of Camelot and the New Frontier, the man with the idealistic promises of his June 10, 1963, speech at American

University and his June 26, 1963, speech at Brandenburg Gate in front of a divided Berlin. The Kennedy legacy is synonymous with the America of the mid-20th century, infused with bold optimism, service to country, and reaching for one's highest potential in the face of a nuclear arms race with a Soviet nemesis that could lead to Armageddon.

The Murrow brand at USIA holds its prominent place too these fifty years later. Murrow's public diplomacy personality—as reflected in his USIA speeches and commentary that follow—is to be serious in professional goals and objectives, but to not take himself too seriously. Murrow often jokingly referred to himself as the Satchel Paige of the Kennedy administration, a nod to the legendary right-handed Negro League pitcher who was the oldest rookie at the age of 42 to play Major League Baseball. Nominated at age 52, Murrow was nine years senior to the 43-year-old Kennedy, whose cabinet consisted of many contemporary 30- and 40-somethings in contrast to the 50-somethings who dominated the Eisenhower administration. Murrow's deputies who helped him run USIA were Donald W. Wilson and Thomas C. Sorensen, both in their mid-30s at the time of their appointments. George Stevens Jr. was 29 when he left Hollywood in 1962 where he was working with his famous director father, George Stevens (**Giant, A Place in the Sun**). Murrow had invited the younger George to produce documentary films at USIA as the head of the Agency's Motion Picture Division. Though junior was hesitant to make the move from Hollywood to Washington, senior told his son, "You **have** to do it."[17] David McCullough, who would rise to become one of America's preeminent historians, was still in his 20s when he worked as an editor of magazines at USIA.

Murrow's elder status among Kennedy appointees, his passionate convictions, and speechmaking abilities made him a favorite among all the Kennedy appointees and led to invitations to speak regularly across the United States. It is estimated that while Murrow was at USIA he received hundreds of speaking requests per week, but turned down all but one or two in order to balance his day-to-day public service duties with his broader commitment to inform and explain USIA to a domestic audience. What drove him to speak over and over was eternal frustration with the lack of government resources. Murrow was famously repelled by financial or administrative matters and despised the hat-in-hand approach needed to get and keep appropriations flowing for his Agency.

Despite his brand renown, Murrow could not obtain a consistent increase in congressional appropriations throughout his three years in Kennedy's administration and a June 1963 speech reflects his weariness. He forthrightly told a gathering of the American Advertising Federation in Atlanta, "Either the House of Representatives believes in the potency of ideas and the importance of information or it does not. And on the record, it does not so believe."[18] His domestic speeches helped to build better understanding about how USIA functions overall in the U.S. foreign policy process. He viewed the U.S. citizen taxpayer, like I did thirty years later, as the main client to USIA, even though the target audience was strictly global. Like JFK, Murrow's federal government service was one thousand days. His health was very poor by the time he officially departed federal service just a few months after Kennedy's assassination in Dallas. His death a year later prevented him from having a third act in his life, what may have been more public service as a U.S. senator or ambassador if his friends and supporters had their way. More likely is that he would have written his memoirs. Now we'll forever know him as a man whose life was cut short in time but was very long in memory.

With John P. Cosgrove

Chapter 2

Brand Murrow

The truth is rarely pure and never simple.
     Oscar Wilde

Egbert Roscoe Murrow has been dead for nearly half a century. Better known as Edward R. Murrow, he was born to farming Quakers in Guilford County, North Carolina, on April 25, 1908, and passed away from lung cancer at his Glen Arden Farm estate in Pawling, New York, on April 27, 1965. Raised in the Tar Heel State in a modest log cabin home with no electricity or running water, his ashes were scattered in an Empire State garden an hour's drive north of Manhattan. His father, a farmer, never did quite "get" his son's profession. "My father did not go so far as to say there's something dishonest about a man making a living merely by talking. But he did think there's something doubtful about it."[19]

As he once said about Abraham Lincoln's legacy, Edward R. Murrow's fifty-seven years and two days "have yet to end."[20] Upon hearing of his death, President Lyndon B. Johnson called Murrow a "gallant fighter" who "dedicated his life both as a newsman and as a public official to the unrelenting search for truth."[21] The spirit and moral conscience of what makes for the best journalism—truth telling and truth seeking—is very much alive in Brand Murrow.

No one in American broadcast journalism in the 20th century was as revered as Murrow. Walter Cronkite was his living room doppelganger, though Cronkite was a news anchor first—king of all anchormen—and a reporter second. Murrow was first, and always, a news reporter who bucked the system. He did not sit well or long behind a desk and often assumed yes before the executives or sponsors could say no. Murrow and Cronkite were legendary competitors at CBS who remained at odds over their distinct journalistic styles. Murrow tried to recruit Cronkite in the 1940s to join his team of young broadcast journalists covering Europe during World War II, but Cronkite turned him down and remained at United Press International.[22] Though born in the South and educated in the Pacific Northwest at a state college (today's Washington State University), Murrow was more erudite and Northeast Ivy League in demeanor and delivery. Cronkite was a University of Texas dropout with the everyman voice of Middle America Missouri, from whom anyone of a certain age can recall hearing "Uncle Walter" deliver the solemn news of a president cut down by an assassin's bullet. When Cronkite died in 2009, Brian Williams, anchor of NBC Nightly News, told Time magazine, "We loved him because he was one of us. He was the voice of America. He was the best there ever was."[23] Murrow could similarly be characterized as the "best there ever was" but he was not, like Cronkite, "one of us" since he was the closest thing to God to carry a microphone.[24]

Both men shared a reputation for credibility through objectivity, which, in the American journalism profession connotes a certain neutral acceptance of just the facts, as in Cronkite's sign-off, "And that's the way it is," and Murrow's opening, "This ... is London." It is a form of descriptive journalism more than the advocacy journalism typical of op-ed pieces and bloggers today. That reputation for "just the facts" changed for Cronkite in 1968 when he editorialized a negative prognosis for the war in Vietnam, which—legend would have it—helped to drive President Johnson from seeking reelection.[25] It changed for Murrow in 1961 in a dramatic fashion when he left CBS to head the government propaganda agency, USIA, at the invitation of President John F. Kennedy.

No one in American journalism in recent years can compare to the hagiographic record of Edward R. Murrow, even if a few television journalists like Ted Koppel and Bill Moyers draw favorable comparisons and others like Keith Olbermann, Tim Russert, or Peter Jennings draw milder comparisons.[26] Brand Murrow remains intact and exalted, like a precious jewel in a box on a shelf for displaying at special times during the year. These special occasions are called Edward R. Murrow Awards. A Murrow Award can mean a number of things. Since 1971, the Radio Television Digital News Association

(RTDNA), formerly the Radio-Television News Directors Association (RTNDA) has awarded the Edward R. Murrow Awards for excellence in electronic journalism. In 2010, 59 news organizations received 89 Murrow awards with NBC News receiving the award for Overall Excellence in its 2009 coverage, including its coverage of the inauguration of President Barack Obama.

Murrow's alma mater, Washington State University, home to the Murrow School of Communication, gives out Edward R. Murrow Awards to the most prominent broadcast journalists.[27] The Fletcher School of Law and Diplomacy at Tufts University in Massachusetts, home since 1965 to the Edward R. Murrow Center of Public Diplomacy, awards the Edward R. Murrow Award for Excellence in Public Diplomacy to a U.S. State Department employee. In 2006, the U.S. State Department initiated the Edward R. Murrow Program for Journalists, a public-private venture with the Aspen Institute and leading journalism schools across the country such as the Manship School of Mass Communication at Louisiana State University and the S.I. Newhouse School of Public Communications at Syracuse University. Included in the itinerary of the International Visitor Leadership Program, the Murrow Program for Journalists is part of the post-9/11 public diplomacy strategy to introduce up-and-coming foreign journalists to American journalistic principles of free speech and a free press. As of 2012, the program had nine partner journalism and communication schools that host the visiting foreign journalists as part of their three-week tour of the United States.[28]

Not to be outdone by private media, the government, or the academy, since 1977 the Corporation for Public Broadcasting has given the Edward R. Murrow Award for Outstanding Contributions to Public Radio.[29] Past recipients include National Public Radio's longtime legal affairs correspondent, Nina Totenberg, and Ira Glass, host and executive producer of "This American Life." The international press in America plays its part too. The Overseas Press Club of America awards the Edward R. Murrow Award for Best TV Interpretation or Documentary on Foreign Affairs. Two outstanding journalism watchdog groups, the Committee of Concerned Journalists and the Reporter's Committee for Freedom of the Press, acknowledge

Murrow's legacy in their activities and programs. The Council on Foreign Relations awards an annual Edward R. Murrow Press Fellowship to a foreign correspondent or editor with a grant from the CBS Foundation. The list goes on and on for this North Star in American journalism.

In his lifetime, Murrow was regularly recognized for his twenty-five years of groundbreaking journalism at Columbia Broadcasting Systems (CBS). On September 14, 1964, President Johnson presented Murrow with the Medal of Freedom, our nation's highest civilian honor, with this statement: "A pioneer in education through mass communication, he has brought to all his endeavors the conviction that truth and personal integrity are the ultimate persuaders of men and nations." On that day Murrow shared the dais with fellow Medal of Freedom recipients Helen Keller, Carl Sandburg, John Steinbeck, and Walter Lippmann.

Just a little over a month before his death, on March 5, 1965, Queen Elizabeth II named him Honorary Knight Commander of the Order of the British Empire, an honor shared with the likes of U2 musician Paul "Bono" Hewson and Bob Hope and fellow countrymen Steven Spielberg and Billy Graham. All of these men share in common the gift of being global persuaders, whether through religion, entertainment, music, or film. They also are recognized as global humanitarians whose work elevates our better selves. In Murrow's case, with the exception of music, he led in all categories. He was multimedia and cross platform before such words existed. Objectivity notwithstanding, he retained a lifelong reputation as a great liberal crusader against bigotry and overzealousness, and outspoken advocate for the downtrodden and disenfranchised. He also fit into the category of international celebrity, a label that he was less famously known for shunning.

He talked to Monroe and Bogart in "Person to Person," what some called "Murrow Lite," but also challenged the intellect in his earlier programs, "Small World," "Hear It Now," and "See It Now." He gave hope to a continent terrorized by goose-stepping militia and comforted an island nation under fire from Nazi bombers. His final television projects for CBS were "Who Speaks for Birmingham?" and "Harvest of Shame," both of which are considered classics in provocative documentary style.

Murrow had many would-be trademarks throughout his broadcasting career: the tall, dark and handsome brooder with his omnipresent cigarette, furrowed brow and cocked head, straightforward news delivery, intellectualizer ("Egghead" Murrow), all of which conjure up the picture of the pinnacle in American newsmen. Ask anyone who is old enough to remember his visage on CBS television and many will recall one of these trademark features of a man who is long gone but too impressionable to forget. We long for his likeness—perhaps without the cigarette—because it's so easy to take umbrage at the state of media today, most specifically hard news, which seems overtaken by soft news and water cooler gossip. We need our gumshoe journalist superhero, pen as sword, to come down from the heavens to zap out frivolous commentary or celebrity idolatry, but we keep searching in vain and wondering WWMS (What Would Murrow Say) or WWMD (What Would Murrow Do). This may explain why Murrow's journalistic ghost continues to hover in some usual and unusual places.

Murrow is perhaps best known in entertainment culture for the 2005 Oscar-nominated film, **Good Night, and Good Luck,** which includes George Clooney as CBS News president Fred Friendly. Clooney also directed and co-wrote the film. The film explores the confrontation between Murrow and ardent anti-Communist Senator Joseph McCarthy (R-WI), whose tactics were attacked by Murrow in a program called "A Report on Senator Joseph R. McCarthy" that aired on "See It Now" on March 9, 1954. One month later McCarthy was allowed to critique Murrow's program in an uninterrupted presentation on April 6, 1954. David Strathairn plays the role of Edward R. Murrow, for which he received an Oscar nomination for best actor, one of six Oscar nominations for the film.

The phrase "Good night and good luck" is as closely associated with the CBS brand Murrow as the war correspondent phrase, "This ... is London." Keith Olbermann, former host of MSNBC's "Countdown" program, who has often referred to Edward R. Murrow as his journalistic hero, regularly ended his show with Murrow's famous goodbye. In 2008, Prime Minister José Luis Rodríguez Zapatero of Spain invoked Murrow's words, "Good night and good luck" during a televised debate among candidates. When asked why he used the phrase, Zapatero said that the phrase "was a hymn to freedom of speech, a sensible denunciation to those who discredit and insult whoever doesn't think like them, have different beliefs, fight for freedom or report disloyalties, those who take in, those who feel, who believe and dream." Zapatero, member of the Spanish Socialist Workers' Party, was reelected for a second term.

The Murrow brand is best associated with a Tiffany Network legacy of the highest quality in American television news journalism never to be seen again. Veteran band Fleetwood Mac released its 2003 album, "Say You Will," on which the second track written by Lindsey Buckingham is called "Murrow Turning Over in His Grave." Though impossible, given Murrow's cremation, the lyrics are meant to indict the state of media today: "Murrow's turnin' over in his grave. Ed Murrow had a child the damn thing went wild." Given Murrow's strong reputation for principled journalism, he is undoubtedly spinning on a regular basis.[30] In the film, **The Insider**, producer Lowell Bergman of CBS "60 Minutes" (Al Pacino) is confronted by reporter Mike Wallace (Christopher Plummer) after a proposed exposé on the tobacco industry is edited down to suit CBS corporate and legal. Wallace shows a **New York Times** editorial to Bergman, which Wallace says, "…accuses us of betraying the legacy of Edward R. Murrow."

The CBS situation comedy series finale of **Murphy Brown** had the television journalist Murphy (Candice Bergen) meeting Edward R. Murrow in heaven and included archival footage of Murrow. **Murphy Brown** made a number of references to Murrow in its ten-year run. Anchorman Jim Dial (Charles Kimbrough) refers to Murrow and other news legends when lamenting the state of modern media. Jim asks, "What would Edward R. Murrow say?" "What would Eric Sevareid say?" to which Corky Sherwood (Faith Ford) responds, "They wouldn't say anything, Jim. You know why? Because they're dead!"

Murrow's reputation for credibility explains his role as narrator of a military propaganda film, *The Challenge of Ideas*, produced by the U.S. Army Pictorial Center. In the spirit of the Frank Capra *Why We Fight* series of World War II, this Cold War film was designed to educate service members about the ideological and information war between the U.S. and U.S.S.R., as well as the moral and spiritual supremacy of the American way of life over its superpower nemesis. Other featured narrators are David Brinkley, John Wayne, Lowell Thomas, Jack Webb, and Helen Hayes. Murrow also played himself in recreated broadcasts for the WWII-themed Hollywood film, *Sink the Bismarck!* Even Warner Bros. caught the Murrow fever in a cartoon short, "Person To Bunny," that featured Bugs Bunny, Daffy Duck, and Elmer Fudd in a parody of Murrow's "Person to Person." The knock-off interviewer, Cedric R. Burrows, is seen seated with his back to the audience enveloped in a cigarette cloud.

With so much fanfare for Murrow's legacy in journalism, why so little documentation of Murrow's second, albeit short career in public information advocacy, a.k.a., the American propaganda business? First and foremost, Murrow's tenure at the United States Information Agency was marred by illness. A lifelong smoker whose habit was up to sixty-five regular unfiltered Camel brand cigarettes a day, he suffered from chronic bouts of pneumonia and persistent coughs, including repeated visits to the hospital. One such in-patient episode kept him sidelined during the ten-day Cuban Missile Crisis of October 1962. A shadow on a lung drew scant alarm until one year later he received bad news of a terminal illness. It was late September 1963, barely six weeks before his boss's assassination in Dallas, Texas. Doctors found a malignant tumor in his left lung and said that operating was futile. Though President Lyndon B. Johnson asked him to stay on, Murrow chose to resign from USIA in January 1964. He would die fifteen months later.

But just as compelling as his poor health in his last years, the image of Brand Murrow as the most dedicated journalist in search of and reporting about the truth is not in complete harmony with either his broadcasting career at CBS or his service as America's chief propagandist. To Murrow, truth and propaganda were cohabitating in a representative democracy like the United States, but their union, like Felix and Oscar of *The Odd Couple*, was often at odds. The neat and tidy Felix was the truth in a country that touted freedom and the First Amendment, while the sloppy Oscar was more like propaganda in a democracy—never clean in either theory or practice. Murrow's lingering brand, illustrated by all those Murrow awards, is one of objectivity, aligned more with the truth end of the information spectrum, while opinion and advocacy lie at the other end. Murrow certainly exalted the principle of objectivity in journalism.

A purely objective position asserts that journalists are never to stray across the line of separation between telling the facts and advocating a personal agenda. He was not a purist, however, especially when he shifted from strictly reporting duties. He explained the job of a news analyst at the conclusion of his first weekday radio broadcast, "Edward R. Murrow and the News," an evening radio broadcast for CBS News that ran from 1947 to 1959. This is a long entry but it is a stunning revelation to a listening audience because Murrow explains what his contractual obligations are and how he might take some liberty with them. It is Monday, September 29, 1947:

> I should like to say a personal word about this series of broadcasts. Perhaps the best way to do it is to read you a paragraph from my contract. It says that news programs are broadcast "solely for the purpose of enabling the listeners thereto to know facts—so far as they are ascertainable—and so to elucidate, illuminate and explain facts and situations as fairly as possible to enable the listener to weigh and judge for himself. In other words, Columbia endeavors to assist the listener in weighing and judging developments throughout the world, but refrains particularly with respect to all controversial, political, social and economic questions from trying to make up the listener's mind for him. News periods should be devoted to giving the facts emanating from an established news-gathering source, to giving all the color in the proper sense of the word,

and interest, without intruding the views of the analyst. The news-analyst further can, and very often should, give us as much light as possible on the meaning of events; the news-analyst should not say they're good or bad in his opinion but should analyze their significance in the light of known facts, the results of similar occurrences and so on. And in this he, of course, should always be fair. He is fully entitled to give, and should give, the opinions of various persons, groups or political parties when these are known, leaving the listener to draw his own conclusions after he has been, as well as possible, informed about the event, its meaning, the attitude of persons or groups toward it, and the known results of similar things in the past."

Now that's pretty complicated language, the kind that lawyers like to write. My own interpretation of it is that this program is not a place where personal opinion should be mixed up with ascertainable facts. We shall do our best to identify sources and to resist the temptation to use this microphone as a privileged platform from which to advocate action.

It is not, I think, humanly possible for any reporter to be completely objective, for we are all to some degree prisoners of our education, travel, reading—the sum total of our experience. And we shall try to remember that the mechanics of radio which make it possible for an individual voice to be heard throughout the entire land don't confer great wisdom or infallibility on that individual. [31]

It is this "prisoner" mentality that guided Murrow when he came on board at a U.S. government propaganda agency. He would not be completely objective, not when it came to promoting the cause of the United States of America over that of the Soviet Union. This was a tough assignment for the new propagandist, given the absolutist narrative advantage a totalitarian state had over a free-for-all representative democracy, but he would use his brand recognition from his reporting days to speak directly to the American people about his new job and its purpose.

Murrow at a press conference

Chapter 3

The Murrow Narrative

While his entire professional reputation for objectivity stood in support of telling the truth and letting the facts lead the story telling, Murrow's government foreign affairs service beckoned him, like a ship's siren, toward the rockier slopes of advocacy and ideological persuasion. Sometimes the landing was softer, while at other times his credibility took a beating. The best illustration for the latter is his wrong-headed opposition to the broadcasting of his former employer's "Harvest of Shame" special overseas on the BBC network, an embarrassing episode he said in hindsight when he forgot which hat he was wearing. He became much more of an ideological crusader in how he explained the role of the United States Information Agency in the many speeches and statements he gave as a government official. The speeches are not diatribes or polemics, and are actually full of Murrow's famous self-deprecating humor despite their serious tone. They also reveal a man of strong convictions who wanted his compatriots and those who held the federal purse strings to understand the paramount importance that ideas and overseas actions played as non-lethal weapons in the new Kennedy administration.

On March 14, 1961, during his nomination statement before Congress he said this about the Cold War between the United States and the USSR: "No man can set either a time limit or dollar limit upon this contest between the forces of freedom and those who would demean and brutalize mankind. The contest will be prolonged and it will cost much treasure. There is no guarantee we will win it. If we should lose, it will be by default, and history will take its revenge."[32] Two years later he was still banging the drum of advocacy in an environment of truth that a representative democracy stood for, always in principle, and often in practice:

> As long as the U.S. Government has been engaged in this activity, and that is more than 21 years, there has been confusion about the role of "truth" in a government information program. But there is no confusion within USIA, nor has there been for many years. We operate on the basis of truth. Voice of America news broadcasts are balanced and objective. They cover all the news, even when it hurts.
>
> American traditions and the American ethic require us to be truthful, but the most important reason is that truth is the best propaganda and lies are the worst. To be persuasive we must be believable; to be believable we must be credible; to be credible we must be truthful. It is as simple as that.[33]

Murrow did not want to be out of the loop, rather, inside the Beltway consciousness from the start. His most famous quote during his USIA service in Washington, "Dammit, if they want me in on the crash landings, I'd better damned well be in on the takeoffs," is a reference to his being left out of the information war side of the Bay of Pigs action during the first few months of the Kennedy administration.[34] He requested and gained his seat at the national policy table and here he was dedicated to the premise that the United States version of the truth was the best propaganda. Such truth included exalting a more sanitized story of America programming for an overseas audience in opposition to the big lies that the Soviets were telling. For its part, Moscow's *Pravda* made much hay about the *CBS Reports* "Harvest of Shame" debacle led by the American journalist-turned propagandist who built up his legend as "Mr. Integrity."[35]

The *New York Times* laid down primer paint for Murrow's iconic legacy when it reported about his multimedia achievements and independent streak in a 3,864-word obituary published three days after his death, its heading like a Times Square news ticker:

"Edward R. Murrow, Broadcaster And Ex-Chief of U.S.I.A., Dies"

> Mr. Murrow achieved international distinction in broadcasting, first as a radio correspondent reporting from London in World War II and then as a pioneer television journalist opening the home screen to the stimulus of controversy. No other figure in broadcast news left such a strong stamp on both media.
>
> In an industry often given to rule by committee, Mr. Murrow was always recognized as an individual, whether in the front lines of the war, in the executive conferences of a network or, in what he enjoyed most, in planning his next story. His independence was reflected in doing what he thought had to be done on the air and worrying later about the repercussions among sponsors, viewers and individual stations.

One of "Murrow's Boys" at CBS, Howard K. Smith, called Edward R. Murrow "the most impressive male person I was ever to know." (He added, "The most impressive female person I ever met I married.") Smith describes Murrow's political influence:

> Along with Ernie Pyle and William Shirer he was one of the three outstanding journalists of World War II. Millions waited on his broadcast each day. His reports on the British, under fire and alone, surely helped move Americans from neutrality to the angels' side. Whenever he returned to the U.S. for a short spell, he was called to the White House for consultation with Roosevelt. He was probably even more popular in Britain, where his pieces were rebroadcast and were a factor in sustaining morale. Churchill, himself a master of language, was an ardent listener and called him a master of language.[36]

Lynne Olson, author of *Citizens of London: The Americans Who Stood with Britain in its Darkest Hour*, identifies Murrow as the most famous American in wartime London. She describes the enormous persuasive influence that his broadcasts had on American listeners when he was seen as the most credible journalist in international news broadcasting:

> If he implied, as he did more and more often, that England couldn't go it alone, that America would have to join the fight, well, maybe he was right, many in his audience thought. Hundreds of Americans wrote him to say his broadcasts had taken them from neutral detachment to support for the British. In September 1940, a Gallup Poll reported that 39 percent of Americans favored providing more U.S. aid to Britain. One month later, as bombs fell on London, and Murrow brought the reality of it into American living rooms, 54 percent thought more aid should be sent.[37]

Murrow's 25-year career at CBS spanned the domination of radio broadcasting in the late 1930s through World War II to the rise of television in the 1950s. Having honed his velvet baritone voice and descriptively dramatic rhetorical style on radio, he did not embrace television at first blush. "I wish goddamned television had never been invented,"[38] he once bemoaned to a colleague, and he was prescient, for even today international radio broadcasting is still the dominant medium in international political communication. He later adapted his post-war "Hear It Now" radio broadcasts produced with Fred Friendly to his wildly popular "See It Now" television documentaries that were broadcast on CBS Television from 1951-1958. In its third season, "See It Now" would investigate the rise of McCarthyism in America and divide Murrow's fandom. Critics would view Murrow's McCarthy probe as a sign of his own Communist sympathies, a charge that would reemerge at the time of his USIA nomination.

No journalist today could possibly challenge his employer's corporate authoritarian nature the way Murrow did in his day. He stands alone in American broadcast history as the radio war correspondent who made CBS stand out during World War II. It was his post-war reputation, prestige, and celebrity that gave Murrow autonomous space to do the stories he wished, corporate resistance and budget be damned. (This attitude did not transfer so well to Washington.) As the *New York Times'* obit reported about Murrow's feelings: "They come to me, the vice presidents, and say, 'Look, there's so much going out of this spout and only so much coming in.' And I say, 'If that's the way you want to do it, you'd better get yourselves another boy.'"[39]

Without his venerable position in the media company, it is highly doubtful that CBS brass would have ventured toward subjects like a mock bomb attack on New York City, Joseph McCarthy and the Red Scare, or the plight of migrant farm workers, Murrow's last documentary for the network before moving to Washington to serve under the Kennedy administration. Even the classic, but almost forgotten, *CBS Reports* "Who Speaks for Birmingham?" was an uncredited Murrow vehicle that his colleague Howard K. Smith took over and finished after Murrow left CBS for government service.[40] Murrow had conducted many of the initial interviews with Birmingham citizens in January 1961, just a few days before the announcement of his appointment to head USIA went public.[41]

For Murrow, in the beginning, and forever after, was the word. It began with his mother's Quaker teachings as a boy in North Carolina to his college years in the Pacific Northwest, where he studied speech communication and rhetoric after switching from the major of business at Washington State College in Pullman. Here he met his favorite professor and mentor from whom he took what can only be called a supernova course overload, nineteen speech classes with Professor Ida Louise Anderson. It is Anderson who honed his speech to its famous affect, down to the pregnant pause in "This ... is London." She would become another woman of influence in the life of her star pupil, along with his wife and his Quaker mother. This troika is lesser known in the Murrow legacy than that of Murrow with Sorensen and Wilson, but it is equally important in forming a conscientious man oriented toward human discovery, curiosity, and dignity. Murrow described his relationship with Professor Anderson in a letter to his then-fiancée Janet:

> She taught me to love good books, good music, gave me the only sense of values I have.... She knows me better than any person in the world. The part of me that

is decent, wants to do something, be something, is the part she created. She taught me to speak.[42]

As a Phi Beta Kappa graduate in 1930, Murrow headed to New York City where he directed the National Student Federation of America for two years. Murrow took the unpaid job after he gave a memorable speech in Palo Alto, California, at the Fifth Annual meeting of NSFA held that January on the campus of Stanford University. The 21-year old senior speech major from Washington State College held his own among other luminaries who spoke, including George Creel, Woodrow Wilson's propaganda czar and head of the Office of War Information. While Creel spoke on "The Power of Opinion," Murrow rose to encourage his fellow students to think beyond the three Fs, "fraternities, football, and fun" to affairs of the state and the world beyond.[43]

So impressive was he at NFSA that in short order he was recruited by Stephen Pierce Duggan, founder and director of the worldwide leader in international educational exchange, the Institute of International Education, on whose board of trustees Murrow would remain until his death. The now 23-year-old became Duggan's assistant director, and both would lead the Emergency Committee in Aid of Displaced German Scholars, later the Emergency Committee in Aid of Displaced Foreign Scholars, to help men and women of ideas escape the fascist rise in Europe.[44] By 1935, still in his late 20s, CBS hired him as director of talks and education. His mandate was to explain radio's role in education.

In 1937, just 29 at the time, he was asked by CBS to go to Europe to cover events unfolding, including rumblings toward war. He was a one-man band at first, operating out of London, but traveling extensively throughout the European continent. He soon hired the newspaper writer William Shirer and together they reported back home to America as Hitler's goose-stepping German troops invaded Vienna, Austria. It was those ten days of reporting at the front lines of history unfolding that made Murrow and Shirer household names. His expanded European staff, later dubbed "Murrow's Boys," consisted of Cecil Brown, Charles Collingwood, Richard Hottelet, Larry LeSueur,

Eric Sevareid, and Howard K. Smith. Whenever CBS complained that some of the men didn't sound good on radio, Murrow retorted, "I'm hiring reporters, not announcers." Reporters were supposed to share a narrative that would engage and educate an audience spectrum from truck driver to Ph.D. Murrow told his staff: "You are supposed to describe things in terms that make sense to the truck driver without insulting the intelligence of the professor."[45] His favorite college professor, Ida Lou Anderson, would have been proud of that statement.

Murrow chatting with JFK

Chapter 4

The Ideas Challenger

In late 1960, just before assuming his position as Director of the United States Information Agency, the Army Pictorial Center of the Department of Defense asked Murrow to be the chief narrator of a troop indoctrination film. No more credible a journalistic figure to endorse such a propaganda product could likely be found in those days. "The Challenge of Ideas" was a 30-minute documentary released in summer 1961. It explained to outgoing troops what it was they were fighting for: the American character and the American love for the "freedom and integrity of the individual."[46] The message was simple and direct—the United States pursues individual freedom for all, while the Communist bloc is its polar opposite in seeking worldwide domination by the state. The Soviet state seeks the annihilation of Western freedom. Whichever adversary wins this clash of pursuits will win entirely on the pull of ideas, what today we call soft power:

> The entire globe, even as it trembles in passion with the birth of new nations, and shrinks in the hand of a dispassionate science, is today the site of a momentous conflict. As each side attempts to prove to the world the superiority of its position, the conflict is fought with the words of diplomats, with gestures of friendship and help to uncommitted countries, even with cultural demonstrations. It is fought, indeed, on every level of man's experience, for the stakes are high. As one of the adversaries in the conflict, we see a challenge as great as any in our historic past, a challenge not we hope to be met and joined in battle, but to be faced in the hearts and hopes of men. It is the challenge of ideas.[47]

"The Challenge of Ideas" was a replacement film for two anti-Communism training films that were pulled by the Department of Defense for being too heavy-handed, bombastic, and conspiratorial in their narrative. The House Committee on Un-American Activities (HUAC) produced "Operation Abolition" and "Communism on the Map" was produced privately by conservative Christian Harding College (now Harding University) of Arkansas. "Operation Abolition" showed scenes from a college student demonstration in downtown San Francisco at one of the HUAC hearings. Though the students were there to call for the abolishment of HUAC, the Committee chose to use select scenes from the protests to identify known Communists, with the intended guilt-by-association implication that college campuses in the 1960s were a hotbed for Communist sympathizers.

"Communism on the Map" implies that the U.S. was being slowly but surely encircled by Communist ideology, aided and abetted by figures like General George C. Marshall and FDR who allowed China to go Communist, and foreign influence from the British Labor Government. Even the majority of NATO member states like France, Sweden and Norway are accused of being composed mainly of socialist and communist leaders. [48] The National Education Program (NEP), founded by Harding College president Dr. George S. Benson, produced the film. NEP's goal was to promote American patriotism, the free enterprise system and crusade against Communism both at home and abroad. Benson was quite popular with strongly anti-Communist groups like the John Birch Society. As his popularity grew, Benson received media profiles that celebrated his mission: "If I Were a Communist" in *Reader's Digest* and "Arkansas Crusader" in *The Saturday Evening Post*.[49]

Both films were seen as too religious right in their viewpoint, reminiscent of the Red Scare of the 1950s, and much too sophomoric for an audience of young fighting men. Once released for public showing, "Operation Abolition," which featured many Cal-Berkeley students, became a cult classic, where, depending on ideological orientation, viewers would either heckle and boo at some of its obviously conspiratorial scenes or praise its warnings.[50] The

American Civil Liberties Union of Northern California sponsored its own response film to correct the film's false accusations that it dubbed "Operation Correction."[51]

Because of all the controversy surrounding these two films, the Department of Defense withdrew them and replaced their rightist slant with "The Challenge of Ideas," seen as much more balanced and middle-of-the-road in its presentation. American servicemen could learn about America's heritage and how and why it was being threatened by Soviet ambition. Unlike the other training films that focused so much on America's soft underbelly—Communist threats from within the United States—Murrow's film focused on the Soviet threat beyond our shores. Included in Murrow's more sophisticated propaganda film were stage and screen actors Helen Hayes and John Wayne; journalist Hanson W. Baldwin, military editor for *The New York Times*; NBC news analyst Frank McGee; and commentator Lowell Thomas. Everything about "The Challenge of Ideas" was Murrowesque in style, including his direct and measured engagement with the audience:

> I'm Edward R. Murrow. For a little while, I would like to review with you the great conflict of our times, one which demands and must get the attention and the involvement of each one of us. This conflict is the reason why most of you are in uniform and some of you will be going overseas: servicemen, families of servicemen, and civilians working for the Department of Defense. Because of this conflict, many of you are already abroad, more than a million Americans in ninety-one foreign countries.
>
> And the conflict itself, how can it be defined? Well, let's look at it this way. The Communist bloc would like to see the entire world under Communist domination.
>
> It is not a conflict between peoples, but between basic values and systems of government. Between the

> principles of life each believes in. When we talk of these conflicting values, we are obliged to speak of that special quality which we call, for want of a better phrase, individual liberty. And when we talk of this liberty in America, we talk with many voices, for we are a diverse nation, and there are perhaps as many concepts of what America is as there are people among us.[52]

While many associated with "Operation Abolition" and "Communism on the Map" would view a left-leaning journalist like Edward R. Murrow to be too soft on communism and socialism, there is clear evidence in Murrow's USIA speeches that Murrow took his crusading role at the United States Information Agency very seriously. He clearly identifies global communism and the Soviet Union as the greatest threats to American freedom. This Murrow—that of the propagandist and bureaucrat—is not the Murrow in the collective memory of many journalists and students of journalism today. But as far as Murrow was concerned, his three years of government service to his country was his most important public mission: "I now think I really understand the process of decision making in this governmental structure of ours, and I am sure I did not understand it at all before I got involved in it."[53]

Swearing in of George Stevens, Jr., head of the Motion Pictures Division

Chapter 5

Mania for Murrow

In late January 1961 when Edward R. Murrow's appointment as the new director of the United States Information Agency was announced, it was met with much anticipation about his ability to perform at the same high level as he had at Columbia Broadcasting System for a quarter century.

Jo Sales of New York's *Journal-American* wrote that Murrow was "the image of CBS in the minds of millions of listeners and viewers. To replace Murrow was virtually impossible, according to seasoned hands at CBS. It was like trying to come up with another Babe Ruth, another Elmer Davis, another Robert Sherwood."[54] Murrow's talent was to serve not only as a great newsman, he also had the ability to act as chief of social conscience for the entire industry. In a speech he gave to the Radio and TV Executives Society shortly before his USIA appointment, Murrow noted the decline in his field of mass media and the rise of one-newspaper cities, calling on a National Information Institute to address the problem.[55] Some press reports wondered how American journalism would even survive the loss of its most esteemed member.

> The appointment of Edward R. Murrow to head the United States Information Agency may be well and good, even considering Mr. Murrow's well-known distaste for things administrative or executive. He is an idea man whose every word is drama. But where does this leave the field of private editorial broadcasting?
>
> The need is greater than ever for examination in detail of national and world questions today. Whiz kids are not a substitute for editorial depth. The truth is that since the death of Elmer Davis, and probably even

before, beginning with the end of World War II, the field of commentators has been narrowing when it should be expanding; and when, paradoxically radio is shifting more and more to "news," along with music, under the impact of teevee.[56]

The *Lexington Dispatch* celebrated its favorite son who followed the information agency leadership of Durham, North Carolina, native George V. Allen:

> No doubt it will be quite pleasing to many North Carolinians who are aware of the fact that Mr. Murrow is a former Greensboro newspaperman who has made an international reputation in the field of television and formerly was regarded as one of the leading radio broadcasters. Murrow is regarded as a man with original ideas and not merely a capable reader of prepared and strictly limited copy.[57]

For the record, Murrow was a native of the Greensboro area but had never been a newspaperman, much less in Greensboro. The *Harrisburg News* of Pennsylvania said that Murrow's succeeding George V. Allen at USIA "could be stimulating to watch. A cloud of smoke…a solemn face…the sonorous voice—'This is Washington.' And the world will have met the Oracular American."[58] The Pine Bluff *Commercial* was breathless: "The appointment of Edward R. Murrow to head the United States Information Agency is such a good appointment as to constitute something of a shock. The government just never fits a man to a job with such precision."[59]

Major media market newspapers played up Murrow's leaving CBS at the height of his power. The *New York Post* reported Murrow's steep pay cut to $21,000 per year as well as frustrations with his employer's "restrictions on reporting and news comments. It is believed they would be glad to go with him to USIA. The CBS news organization has been under pressure since the National Conventions last July, when ratings showed NBC outscored them by a wide margin. At that time Murrow was rushed in to team with Walter Cronkite but the result was not altogether happy."[60]

Cecil Smith of the *Los Angeles Times* echoed this sentiment:

> The abdication of Edward R. Murrow from his TV-radio pinnacle to head the U.S. Information Service came at a rather curious time. A few years ago, Ed was virtually a lone documentary voice crying in the TV wilderness. But he leaves at a time when the air is swamped with documentary and informational programs…As to Murrow's departure, it is no secret that he has not been happy at CBS since the return from his sabbatical. His nose reportedly was far out of joint when he was scheduled to work in tandem this last year with Walter Cronkite—a la Huntley-Brinkley.[61]

The *New York World-Telegram* and *The Sun*, a Scripps-Howard newspaper, identified Murrow at USIA among three "tough jobs" in the Kennedy administration, the two others being Thomas Finletter as representative to NATO and Henry Labouisse, director of foreign aid, then called the International Cooperation Administration (ICA).

> We have one doubt as to Edward R. Murrow in a tough administrative job. It is commonly understood he quit as a TV executive because he didn't fancy administrative work, that he shrank from ever firing anybody—certainly something needed in USIA. He is, however, intimately familiar with world affairs and highly articulate concerning them. This is another area in which we often have bought far too little for our money.
>
> There is no doubt Mr. Murrow has the "feel" for this sort of interpretive, even evangelistic, assignment. The question is his ability to make over a far-flung organization into something more effective. We certainly wish him well.[62]

Conservative-leaning newspapers were not happy with Murrow's appointment. The *Charleston News & Courier* said that the choice of Murrow was "surprising but hardly welcome news." While noting Murrow's technical abilities in television documentary production as well as international sophistication, Murrow was a knee-jerk liberal. "That is to say, he is always on the side of those individuals who are passive in the face of Soviet aggression. His view of the so-called underdeveloped countries, for example, is that the U.S. must go more than half way in meeting their demands. The *News and Courier* would prefer as chief of USIA a man with a keen sense of strategic issues in the cold war." [63]

Several papers like *The Atlanta Journal* (now The **Atlanta Journal-Constitution**), the *New York Post* and the *New York Times* played up Murrow's pledge to make the U.S. international information effort based on a "rugged basis of truth." Murrow's wartime reporting reputation hinged on that very effort: he would tell the truth, even when it was not good news or even flattering to the nation.[64]

By far the most significant opining of the day on the subject of Murrow in Washington was a piece, "Policy and Propaganda—Murrow's Assignment," by the influential print commentator James Reston, Washington correspondent for the *New York Times*:

> Edward R. Murrow, the best left-handed putter in Christendom and the most influential reporter of his time, has been given the job of fixing this country's overseas propaganda. Considering the fix it's in, this is quite a job, for no country ever had a better story to tell or failed so lamentably to tell it well as the United States in the sixteen years since the end of the war. This was not because the country did not know the techniques. The United States has spent more time and energy on learning the arts of persuasion than all the countries of the world put together.[65]

Reston wrote that in America a natural aversion to all things propaganda along with cheapskate Congressional appropriations and less than stellar talent at USIA contributed to a poor track record of success. Most of all, USIA staff was never brought in on policy discussions, but left to carry the message of its State Department big brother, without State being advised about the propaganda effect of its worldwide actions.

Take-Offs and Landings

What influences opinion about the United States overseas is not primarily what the United States says but what it does. If it takes sensible policy decisions, carefully considered in propaganda terms before the decisions are released, then an efficient propaganda machine can distribute common sense widely...The question, therefore, is whether Murrow is going to be brought into the policy-making process on the take-offs or only on the crash landings, whether his advice is sought in the National Security Council and the White House on the overseas propaganda effect of questions discussed there, or whether he is to be excluded from questions that clearly affect the nation's propaganda effort.

Rape or Seduction?

The United States Government, however, has not been thinking of overseas information in these terms. It is loud and obvious, preferring rape to seduction. It does not hesitate to spend tens of millions on big splashy propaganda operations when one well-informed $15,000-a-year official working closely with the foreign correspondents in Washington would do the job much better.[66]

Notwithstanding the offensive phrase "preferring rape to seduction" to describe America's overseas information efforts, Reston's words are prescient, for in a few short months, Murrow would experience a harrowing policy crash landing in Cuba. Donald M. Wilson, Murrow's deputy director, was part of the "Troika" of leadership at the Agency along with policy and programs director Tom Sorensen, brother of Kennedy speechwriter and adviser Ted Sorensen. Wilson had been a foreign correspondent for *Life* magazine and received a call on April 12, 1961, from a journalist friend, Tad Szulc, correspondent for the *New York Times*. Szulc had been in Miami where he had been interviewing families of young Cuban-American men who were receiving military training in Nicaragua. It was clear that a military intervention into Cuba was about to occur and with the blessing and backing of the United States. Wilson was shocked to learn that USIA had no forewarning of the intervention. He called Murrow and both set up a meeting immediately with CIA Director Allen W. Dulles. When the story Wilson had heard from Szulc was repeated to Dulles, he neither confirmed nor denied, which in Washington is a confirmation. Murrow was soon summoned to the White House where McGeorge Bundy, Kennedy's National Security Adviser, gave him a briefing about the Bay of Pigs invasion. No one in the U.S. Government was supposed to know about the invasion except for the CIA, which was coordinating the mission. Murrow thought the plan was "the craziest thing he'd ever heard."[67]

Although Murrow was furious about being kept out of the loop, he fulfilled his duties as director of the USIA like a good soldier. His commander-in-chief, Kennedy, took full responsibility and blame for the failed mission, even though the plan was hatched during Eisenhower's last year in office. Wilson recalls Murrow's loyalty to Kennedy:

> Although there were other people in the government who were quick to say, "I told you so," Murrow kept his mouth shut after the invasion. He never said another word to Bundy, the president, or anyone else about his personal feelings on the matter. This behavior is a very valuable quality in any administration and it endeared him to Kennedy.[68]

Roles are reversed as Murrow is interviewed by budding Ghanaian journalists in Accra on January 13, 1962

Chapter 6

Murrow, Kennedy, and Controversy

When Murrow transitioned from journalist to propagandist, he maintained his devotion to the word. A good story was best told facts forward, even if he had to now package those facts with America's good intentions. Whether the news about America was good or bad, Kennedy's chief persuasive tactician would choose a balanced interpretation of the truth over heavy-handed propaganda. This is exactly what Kennedy attracted, and got, for the job: an oppositionist by nature in the form of a devoted public servant.[69]

John F. Kennedy wanted a media man of high regard at the helm of the U.S. Information Agency. He should be a high-profile man who would not outshine the president's personal charisma, but who could augment the ideological commitment Kennedy had to countering the Soviet influence. He had that man in Ed Murrow, whose nomination was a shot of adrenaline into the reputation and relevancy of the overseas information agency.

Kennedy aide Thomas Sorensen, who would later become deputy director of the Agency, proposed the following job qualifications:

> Experience in world affairs and knowledge of foreign peoples… Should comprehend the "revolution of rising expectations" throughout the world, and its impact on U.S. foreign policy… Pragmatic, open-minded, and sensitive to international political currents, without being naïve. Understand the potential of propaganda, while being aware of its limitations…[70]

It was, as Alexander Kendrick writes, "an excellent, almost a hand-tooled description of Edward R. Murrow."[71] Sorensen shared Kennedy's commitment to psychological warfare and foreign information programs and thought that Murrow would too with his yin and yang mix of idealism and cynicism. One July 15, 1960, Kennedy's Democratic nomination speech in Los Angeles explained the information war spectrum competition to the American people, what came to be known as "The New Frontier" speech:

> For the harsh facts of the matter are that we stand at this frontier at a turning-point of history. We must prove all over again to a watching world, as we said on a most conspicuous stage, whether this nation, conceived as it is with its freedom of choice, its breadth of opportunity, its range of alternatives, can compete with the single-minded advance of the Communist system.[72]

The names of two CBS newsmen, Dr. Frank Stanton and Edward R. Murrow of "Hear It Now" and "See It Now" fame, were recommended to direct the agency. At first Stanton, president of the Columbia Broadcasting System, seemed an obvious choice given his strong academic and journalistic background, combined with experience in consulting with the Office of War Information, a precursor to USIA. Though offered the job, Stanton declined, not wanting to leave CBS. This shifted immediate attention to the most highly regarded journalist of his day who just happened to want to leave his present employer. Murrow was making well over two hundred thousand a year at CBS, but would accept a 90 percent pay cut—famously promoted during his public service tenure—to become director of America's chief open source propaganda agency. Who was better than the global icon in American journalism, Edward R. Murrow, to tell America's story to the world and make it sound believable? There was no one else with the solid reputation for truth to take on the burdens of an information agency during the Cold War. Once again, his life in words made credible led in the decision to hire Murrow for the job of chief bureaucrat of international information about America.[73]

Murrow's decision to accept the position was surely not an easy one. At 52, he had reached the pinnacle of his broadcasting news profession and mostly on his own terms because he was so good at what he did. He was a veteran war correspondent who had defied company orders from his CBS bosses to refrain from flying military missions during World War II. (He flew 25 missions.) He had directly challenged the Red Baiter Joseph McCarthy and flipped off his own profession with his famous "it is merely wires and lights in a box" speech in 1958 before the Radio and Television News Directors Association.[74] He saw himself as a moral conscience for the nation, not afraid to challenge the power elite in industry and government from Hollywood and Wall Street to the White House and State Department. This champion of the First Amendment—he would posthumously become known as the patron saint of broadcast journalism—elevated his profession from something that takes up that space between advertising, infotainment, and public relations to a point of light in human understanding.

Murrow may have become a cynic about American broadcast journalism, but he was still an idealist about America's stories. He was a true patriot about American values of candidness, fair play, and ingenuity as well as the American way of life. Murrow's own biography, which was regularly shared with both American and international audiences, was an inspiring American story with Horatio Alger clichés. Despite his distinguished Ivy League bearing, Murrow was not born into privilege nor was he educated at a premier institution of higher education. His story was one of great talent, hard work, perseverance, a strong moral foundation, and luck at having been at the right place at the right time. Murrow was now in the right place at the right time to tell America's story in the early 1960s. Who better to unravel the complexities of the country's race relations, its inspiring leaders from Abraham Lincoln to Martin Luther King, than the man who had advocated doing the right thing for London and for Milo. Murrow's story and how he could tell America's story were narratives to share with the world. They could serve as models of development, not one that others had to follow, but to which others could be inspired. The ideological message was simple: America will not impose its will on other nations, but will extend a hand of help and direction without the strings attached of its Soviet competitor.

Before the Kennedy administration, USIA's leadership was not of particular note because the agency was bureaucratically irrelevant to so many. Barely eight years old as an independent agency of the federal government, USIA had no domestic lobby on behalf of its interests, and Congress paid it little heed other than to criticize calls for more appropriations. Previous USIA directors were picked "not because of their competency in a highly professional vocation—that of professional persuading. They were chosen for irrelevant reasons—because they could get along with Congress, or a political debt was being paid off."[75]

With Murrow, Kennedy had a confident man who could advocate foreign confidence in America's foreign policies. But propaganda alone could not substitute for good policies, be they New Frontier initiatives like the Peace Corps, Alliance for Progress in Latin America, or Food for Peace, the latter a rebranding of Public Law 480, the Agricultural Trade Development Assistance Act, that was initiated by Dwight Eisenhower one year after USIA's founding. Kennedy, like Eisenhower and many presidents before him, wanted to combine good policy with good propaganda, but Eisenhower's words often failed to grab headlines the way that Kennedy's could. When Eisenhower signed PL 480 into law in 1954, he said it would "lay the basis for a permanent expansion of our exports of agricultural products with lasting benefits to ourselves and peoples of other lands."[76] Kennedy described the reconstituted legislation Food for Peace in 1961 in direct and simple terms: "Food is strength, and food is peace, and food is freedom, and food is a helping to people around the world whose good will and friendship we want."[77]

Murrow himself had said officially after the Bay of Pigs and "Harvest of Shame" setbacks about USIA that "this Agency with the President recognizes the value of daring and dissent" and greets "healthy controversy as the hallmark of healthy change."[78] Those words from June 1961 show a man who was beginning to warm to his boss in the White House, though he never completely came around to the president at a deep level. In a rare display of personal candor, Murrow later wrote about his impressions of Kennedy in a letter to J. Robert Oppenheimer in 1964:

> I have had great difficulty in trying to reach some judgments regarding that young man's Kennedy's

relations to his time. I saw him at fairly close range
under a variety of circumstances, and there remains for
me a considerable element of mystery—and maybe that
is good. I always knew where his mind was, but I was
not always sure where his heart was.[79]

His enigmatic assessment of his years with Kennedy in Washington reflected an enigmatic relationship with government and politics in general. As a journalist, Murrow had the privilege to cover politicians and their missteps, not be one. His attitude toward government followed a play on the purple cow thesis:

I never was a bureaucrat;
I never hope to see one;
but I can tell you anyhow;
I'd rather see than be one!

He is later to have responded to a friend about his decision: "I had been criticizing bureaucrats all my adult life, and it was my turn to try."[80] Though Murrow may have been ultimately decisive about his decision, the public was not. Morrie Ryskind in the *Los Angeles Times* best reflected the divided public reaction to the announcement of Murrow as head of USIA:

For what comfort it may offer, it may now be
authoritatively said that the violent undulations
registered on our seismographs the last few days
recorded neither an American earthquake of
catastrophic proportions nor a Russian underground
explosion, as was at first feared.

What the delicate machines were noting was the
simultaneous but antithetical reaction of two opposing
forces: (1) the liberal eruption of joy and dancing in the
streets at the news that Edward R. Murrow was to head
the U.S. Information Agency; and (2) the tremors
aroused in the conservative camp by the same news….
The left-of-center response needs little explanation.

> This appointment, to them, definitely puts the right man in the right place. USIA is, basically, our propaganda agency, and, over the years, Mr. Murrow has proven himself to be the foremost propagandist for his cause. The right-wing fears arise from their view that Murrow's cause may not always be the American cause.[81]

Right-wing fears were rampant in 1961 and the White House had its fair share of critical reaction to Murrow's appointment.[82] "My dear Mr. President, Why—why—why Edward R. Murrow to head U.S.I.A.? One must wonder at your faith in this man's ability to expose the Communist conspiracy for what it is—when his record of bias is so well known. Why—why—why could you not have selected a pro-American to stand up for us in this hour of our greatest need?"[83]

Springville Junior High School principal C. Lynn Hanks from Utah sent along a note of concern to President Kennedy, along with a Red Stars No. 3 pamphlet, "The Reds Are Back in Hollywood!!!" "We have been informed, through connections with the F.B.I., that what this pamphlet claims is true and documented and therefore we are wondering why Edward R. Murrow has received such high appointment in our government?"[84] It is not clear in the letter if Murrow is considered a card-carrying Communist or just a hanger-on.

A dentist from Ardmore, Pennsylvania wrote, "It is with extreme regret that I note your selection of Mr. Ed Murrow to head the USIA. This individual with his past record of a front-running apologist for pinko and red tainted situations has not merited the confidence of millions of Americans like myself who still hold to the premise that loyalty is still a virtue."[85]

One of the most supportive letters came from Herbert Beres of Rancho Mirage, California. It reflected the way many liberals felt about Kennedy's information agency selection:

> I have never before written a letter to a public official, but I have never before been so pleased by the

performance of a public official for whom I cast my ballot. It would appear to me that your Administration has begun by appointing to high public office a uniformly high quality of public servant. I am particularly pleased by the announcement today of the appointment of Edward R. Murrow to the head of the U.S. Information Service. Here is one of the very few men in American public life who had the courage to portray the late Senator Joe McCarthy for what he was, a phony and a hypocrite, at the very height of his infamy. For many years Mr. Murrow has been almost the only source of entertaining information and education worth the viewing on commercial television. I applaud you for your wisdom in choosing the perfect man for so important a position.[86]

Another supporter wrote

Mr. Murrow brings to the new administration long experience and a unique competence. He is well known, respected, well traveled and has a sincere feel of the world situation at large. He has known discreetly the past and the present and does have that rare ability to forecast the future with its good and bad effects. These qualities can serve well the Information Agency that can do much to tell the world about us; a truth which we need not hide but should make sure that those who have been denied to know about us and our sincere intentions will now know all.[87]

Others who asked Mr. Kennedy to reconsider the appointment did not share such fulsome praise about Murrow's high qualifications for the post. "A post that important should go to a man of unquestioned patriotism, integrity and judgment." Murrow's appointment was also disquieting to some Arab Americans. Osman Mustafa wrote: "Edward Murrow's appointment as Director of Information is looked upon with extreme disfavor by half a billion Moslems and particularly the Arab world. This is due to his pro Israel stand which for about 15 years has antagonized the entire Moslem world. He therefore was a very unwise choice for the job." Another telegram seems to point to Murrow's comments in his last film for CBS, "Harvest of Shame." "Vigorously protest Murrow's appointment. His low opinion of farmer businessmen in past 'documentaries' should automatically disqualify him. In Cold War of ideas, you have chosen a real loser."

A few telegrams were like Haiku bumper stickers of disgust[88]:

THE PRESIDENT
THE WHITE HOUSE

DO YOU TRUST MURROW AND WHY. I HAVE BEEN WITH YOU SO FAR NOW DOUBTFUL.

****

SCHLESINGER NOW MURROW PATTERN EMERGES ALARMINGLY CLEAR EARNESTLY BESEECH RECONSIDERATION

****

HOW COULD MURROW PROMOTE AMERICAN IDEOLOGY ABROAD HE NEVER EXPOSED COMMUNISTS HERE.

At his nomination hearing, Murrow reflected a change in attitude toward government. In order to be an effective public official who advocated on behalf of America in the world, he had to work closely with the U.S. government and not view it with a jaundiced eye. This Agency director would lead, but only in synch with policies he could support:

> The Agency will attempt to make U.S. policy, as designed by the President, everywhere intelligible and wherever possible, palatable. We shall endeavor to reflect with fidelity to our allies, to the uncommitted nations, and to those who are hostile to us, not only our policy but our ideals.[89]

Murrow's devotion to principled objectivity and the elevation of truth above all would make his three-year tenure as director of the United States Information Agency, if nothing else, memorable. Throughout the Agency's entire lifespan (1953-1999), Murrow would retain his status as the most revered director. But his tenure would also put him smack dab in the middle of those tension-filled intersections we know still today as news journalism versus advocacy communications and the press versus national security.

As a journalist, Murrow believed that describing America's warts and dirty laundry contributed to national understanding. He knew that America's story was not one about a perfect nation or people. No such place or people existed. America's strength was in its historical narrative, ideals, and national conversation. Unlike the Cold War opponents in the Soviet Union and East Germany, the United States of America would never fear showing its true identity—what it was and where it was going. It had much room for improvement in attacking poverty, improving race relations, and confronting political extremism, among many other challenges. This America was always a work-in-progress, as Murrow stated before the House Appropriations Subcommittee, "I think we must assume the attitude that democracy is always unfinished business, and we must never take the attitude that we have reached the complete and final conclusion in all our problems, social, economic, and political."[90]

Would Murrow the propagandist tell the official story of America with a "warts and all" mentality? This is just what conservative-leaning members on Capitol Hill and certain Washington insiders feared the most. He might tip the scale in favor of a picture of America that was too negative. Murrow's reputation as a straight-shooter preceded him, and now it would be tested—not just from the right—but within the corridors of the National Security Council and Kennedy's White House, across the Great Pond to London's BBC, within the Western Hemisphere at the Bay of Pigs, and with Hollywood's left-leaning elite dining at legendary Chasen's restaurant.

In February 1961, the functions and duties of USIA were laid out in a report produced by the U.S. Advisory Commission on Information,[91] a group that had been assessing the overseas information program and making recommendations to Congress since 1948:

> 1. Counsel the Executive Branch on international public opinion by making available its specialized knowledge to [aid in] the formulation and implementation of U.S. foreign policies.
>
> 2. Explain and interpret to people overseas the meaning and purpose of U.S. foreign policies.
>
> 3. Serve as a source of accurate, non-sensational news abroad without competing with U.S. private news sources.
>
> 4. Present the full sweep of American life and culture to the people of the world in order to correct misconceptions and to combat false or distorted pictures of the United States.

The four duties expanded on a March 1959 report that explicitly favored the facts end of the influence spectrum. Back then, the Commission said that USIA should: (1) make clear that its purpose is to inform others about the United States, not try "to persuade them to swap their way of life for ours"; (2) orient information toward a particular audience; and (3) acknowledge that no single program will be suitable around the world.

This vision seemed to clear a straight path for a journalist like Murrow to lead the U.S. Information Agency, given the fact that no one in media worldwide was quite so influential and persuasive as the Murrow of 1961. He was the poster child of credibility for America's storytelling to the world. Murrow told the U.S. Senate Foreign Relations Committee at the time of his nomination that he favored the facts end of the influence spectrum to overt propaganda that packaged information toward the sponsor's ends.[92] "The voice of this country should at all times be steady—firm but not bellicose—carrying the conviction that we will not flinch in the face of threats or provocations."[93]

The United States Government under John F. Kennedy was not averse to propaganda campaigns. At the time of Murrow's appointment, the U.S. was fully engaged in challenging the propaganda machine of the Soviet Union. Murrow, however, believed that in that information war contest, the U.S. must operate "on a basis of truth" in order to have the credibility advantage with the world's people.[94] In a speech to the Radio Television News Directors Association he said, "We not only seek to show people who we are and how we live; but we must also engage others in the delicate, difficult art of human persuasion, to explain why we do what we do."[95]

It was expected that the Soviet Union would distort, lie, and misinform its own people and those it sought to influence around the world. This is a point Murrow makes repeatedly in the speeches that follow. The Soviet system was simple by design because of its totalitarian architecture, while the American system—with its emphasis on criticism and dissent—was much more complex in its delivery. As the leading nation in the free world, the United States had to be careful how it presented its facts to the world because the world expected the country of freedom and free speech ideals to hold itself to a much higher standard than its Communist opponents.

At his nomination hearing, Murrow's reporting point-of-view was challenged by Indiana Republican Senator Homer E. Capehart, who said it was *indeed* USIA's job to sell the United States to the world. Clearly there was a tension between the information and influence range of telling America's story to the world in the 1960s. In the following exchange, Murrow sees credibility as paramount and propaganda (salesmanship) as auxiliary to an effective foreign policy, while Senator Capehart views propaganda as primary to the U.S. cause:

> Senator Capehart: Well, I want to say this: I think you have great ability. I would like to teach you, however, to be a salesman. Maybe you are a good one.

Mr. Murrow: I am not.

Senator Capehart: But my point is that my understanding of your position and of the Agency is that it is to sell the United States to the world, just as a sales manager's job is to sell a Buick or a Cadillac or a radio or television set. Now, I never knew of a salesman who was very successful, or a company that was very successful, that ran in   advertisements and sales stories the weaknesses of their product and the weaknesses of their company. I never knew one like that which was successful. Now, I think I can agree that newspaper reporters must tell the facts as they find them. But isn't this position you are going into the same, in reality, as selling a physical thing? You are selling ideas, are you not? To me it seems to be that.

Mr. Murrow: What I am trying to say is that we cannot be effective in telling the American story abroad if we tell it only in superlatives, if we deny that we have controversies or difficulties, because if we do not report them, they will be reported elsewhere, and the credibility of our reports will thereby be reduced.[96]

Bogota community center

Chapter 7

Murrow Fails an Integrity Test

I yield to no one in my opposition to government efforts to censor free and complete flow of news.
     Edward R. Murrow

On Tuesday, March 14, 1961, Senator Henry M. Jackson of the state of Washington was presenting a favorite son to the Chairman of the Committee on Foreign Relations, Senator J. William Fulbright of Arkansas. Edward R. Murrow was debuting as the prospective next director of the nation's international information agency, USIA.

Though born in Polecat Creek, North Carolina, Murrow had left the southern state as a young boy of six and moved with his family for better economic prospects to the Pacific Northwest. He was educated at Washington State College (now Washington State University) where he became a Phi Beta Kappa in speech communication. By the seventh decade of the 20th century, Murrow had risen to superstar status as America's most well-known and well-recognized broadcast journalist. He was famous and highly regarded outside the United States for his wartime broadcasting, particularly among the British people, who credited him with storytelling prowess as favorably as they did Winston Churchill with his political acumen.

On that late winter morning in 1961, Senator Jackson told Senator Fulbright that Mr. Murrow has a caliber unmatched in government service. "One of the real problems that we face in the cold war is to bring to Government men of the caliber of Mr. Murrow…In my judgment, Mr. Murrow brings to this important agency a high degree of competency and courage. He is a man with a very keen intellect."[97]

Not all the Senate committee members seemed convinced, however, of Mr. Murrow's competency in advocating America's best face in the ideological showdown with the Soviet Union. Would he, in defense of always telling the truth, be inclined to display America's dirty laundry more than its clean wash?

It seemed a fair concern given Murrow's proclivity to host exposé-like CBS documentaries that unveiled America's shortcomings. The last documentary that Murrow produced before taking his USIA position in Washington was "Harvest of Shame," which featured a 29-year-old correspondent named Dan Rather. Its opening statement exposes the dehumanizing ways in which poor, migrant farm workers in the United States were brought to market:

> This scene is not taking place in the Congo. It has nothing to do with Johannesburg or Cape Town. It is not Nyasaland or Nigeria. This is Florida. These are citizens of the United States, 1960. This is a shape-up for migrant workers. The hawkers are chanting the going piece rate at the various fields. This is the way the humans who harvest the food for the best-fed people in the world get hired. One farmer looked at this and said, "We used to own our slaves; now we just rent them."

More than half a century has passed since "Harvest of Shame" aired the day after Thanksgiving in November 1960. Murrow's closing remarks seemed designed to jolt the average American from his soporific holiday feast.

> The migrants have no lobby. Only an enlightened, aroused and perhaps angered public opinion can do anything about the migrants. The people you have seen have the strength to harvest your fruit and vegetables. They do not have the strength to influence legislation. Maybe we do. Good night, and good luck.

The theme of "Harvest of Shame" was a natural swan song for Murrow at CBS. Murrow was known as the champion of the downtrodden. One of his favorite quotes was by Edmund Burke: "The only thing necessary for the triumph of evil is for good men to do nothing," which made his first major blunder at USIA—seeking to censor the media—a bewildering one for his compatriots in the press.

Murrow got wind of the British Broadcasting Corporation's plan to air "Harvest of Shame" on its TV networks. BBC had already paid CBS for the foreign broadcasting rights, but in his new role as chief of America's image overseas, Murrow reached out to BBC Director General Hugh Carleton-Greene to pull the program. He viewed the film's critical portrayal of America's treatment of its own as designed for domestic consumption only and thought it might confuse viewers to his proper role at USIA. The proverbial leak occurred and Murrow had, à la Ricky to Lucy, a lot of 'splainin' to do. How could the poster child of free speech suddenly advocate censorship? It appears he traded in his journalist hat for his propagandist beret, or at least a strong belief at the time that a very high firewall of protection must exist between domestic and global media.

While Murrow defended his intervention, he had to admit later that it was "both foolish and futile."[98] For a time, the controversy seemed to shadow his skyscraper reputation in journalistic integrity.[99] The American Civil Liberties Union sent a telegram expressing alarm:

> Shocked to learn of your almost incredible effort to persuade British Broadcasting officials not to show television documentary on migrant labor situation in the United States. Your quoted explanation in the press that the film was made only for domestic presentation is utterly irrelevant. Your action was attempted official censorship. Unless there is other explanation, our friends and enemies throughout the world can only believe that critical comment in the Senate against content of the film was the cause of your action. Any such subservience will severely damage if not completely destroy at home and abroad the validity of your pledge that USIA policy will be to tell the truth, both good and bad. This principle of freedom of communication should always guide USIA program,

and we urge that you reaffirm and hereafter unmistakably act on this principle.[100]

In response, Murrow gave a two-part answer that spoke to America's great free press tradition but also the need for putting such a program in proper context, which, in Murrow's view, was for domestic use only:

> There is a long and honorable tradition in the literature and journalism of our country, a tradition of social protest and self-examination based upon the belief that democracies' business is always unfinished business. I have tried to work in that tradition for many years. The "Harvest of Shame" was an effort to widen the area of concern and controversy in this country about a matter of very considerable social, economic and educational importance. The American viewer could be expected to look at it in its proper context and not regard it as a portrayal of the total farm situation in the United States. The foreign viewer cannot reasonably be expected to bring the same degree of knowledge or sophistication to the subject. Had I still been employed by CBS, I would have opposed the sale of this particular program abroad.
>
> I was concerned lest my participation in the film might be regarded as somehow reflecting official United States policy, so I did what I have done so often in the past as a private citizen, picked up the phone and made a casual call to Hugh Carlton Greene, the Director General of the BBC. That was an error, but one does not immediately change the habits of 25 years. Nor, I think, is the record of 25 years to be destroyed by one ill-considered call.
>
> I did not act under pressure. I was not requested to make the call by the Senate, the White House, the State Department or anyone else.

> You urge that I "reaffirm and hereafter unmistakably act" on the principle that freedom and communication should always guide the USIA program. I am, of course, happy to do precisely that since it is a principle by which I have tried to live in the past and which I propose to adhere to in the future.[101]

The day after receiving the ACLU telegram, Murrow met with USIA staff in Washington where he received a question about the controversy from the Pakistan language service. The transcript of the proceedings indicates a great deal of support for his mea culpa:

> The question came from the Pakistan Service, direct and penetrating as I have learned to expect from all my friends in Pakistan. How, in view of the fact that there have been two editorials do I view the program, "Harvest of Shame"? I view it, as I did. It was a program produced for domestic consumption. As was suggested in one of the editorials to which you referred, my telephone call was both foolish and futile and that I did not become aware of which hat I was wearing. This may well be an accurate summary. [Loud applause] I hope that in spite of this I shall still have a place to put the hat. [Laughter and applause][102]

In a Q&A session with middle-level diplomats from the Far East in June 1961, USIA Director Murrow had this exchange with one diplomat:

> Foreign Diplomat: I have a personal question, Mr. Murrow. Some weeks ago I read a story to the effect that a television broadcast you made you wanted it to be withdrawn. I saw this broadcast. I thought it was good.
>
> Murrow: I thought it was very good, as a matter of fact. (Laughs)

> Diplomat: I think we don't disagree on that.
>
> Murrow: This was a program I did some months ago before entering government service, which had to do with the quite miserable conditions of migrant laborers in this country. Any viewer in this country could reasonably have been expected to realize that this did not represent the whole spectrum of agricultural labor and its condition in this country, that it represented a very special condition. There is a tradition in this country of journalism—an old and honorable one—which sometimes is called the exposé, sometimes is called muckraking. This was that type of report. The report was honest. Nothing was faked. I objected, on happily failing to realize that I was suddenly speaking for the government rather than as a private citizen. I objected to its being shown abroad as I would have had I still been employed by the Columbia Broadcasting System, which did it; simply because I thought and I still think that the viewer abroad seeing that would have concluded quite erroneously that that was a reflection of the conditions under which many or most agricultural labor in this country labors, and that was the basis for the objection. [103]

Murrow's cautionary note about how readily America's darker narrative should be shared with the world reflects a standard that his boss, the American president, presented in a speech, "The President and the Press," given shortly after the "Harvest of Shame" event occurred. In it, Mr. Kennedy lays out the need for some reportorial balance in coverage due to the formidable ideological opponent at hand. These words are prescient for the surveillance times in which we live with that need to strike the balance between rights and obligations:

> On many earlier occasions, I have said—and your newspapers have constantly said—that these are times that appeal to every citizen's sense of sacrifice and self-

discipline. They call out to every citizen to weigh his rights and comforts against his obligations to the common good. I cannot now believe that those citizens who serve in the newspaper business consider themselves exempt from that appeal.

Every newspaper now asks itself, with respect to every story: "Is it news?" All I suggest is that you add the question: "Is it in the interest of the national security?" And I hope that every group in America—unions and businessmen and public officials at every level—will ask the same question of their endeavors, and subject their actions to the same exacting tests.[104]

Murrow, as was indicated by his USIA staff, did indeed keep his place as the beloved head of the Agency and managed to wear both his journalist and advocate hats, but the "Harvest of Shame" episode was a signifier for how tough it was to transition from beloved keeper of the journalistic flame of integrity to defender of America's image in the world. All things being equal and despite the encroachment of a cold war, Murrow believed that the whole picture of America—warts and all—was the preferable one for a free and independent nation.

VOA 20th anniversary address

Chapter 8

The Murrow Doctrine in Public Diplomacy

If you find faults with our country, make it a better one. If you're disappointed with the mistakes of government, join its ranks and work to correct them. Enlist in our Armed Forces. Become a teacher. Enter the ministry. Run for public office. Feed a hungry child. Teach an illiterate adult to read. Comfort the afflicted. Defend the rights of the oppressed. Our country will be the better, and you will be the happier. Because nothing brings greater happiness in life than to serve a cause greater than yourself.
    John McCain

When William Paley at CBS first hired Edward R. Murrow in 1935 as Director of Talks, it was for public diplomacy purposes and not journalism. Murrow had no journalism experience. He had majored in speech communication at Washington State College. His national stature had grown from his ability to move audiences through words—speeches he gave as president of the National Student Federation of America, and his most recent position as vice president of the Institute of International Education in New York where he worked with President Stephen Duggan to rescue persecuted scholars from a fascist Europe. He was by now a member of the most prestigious foreign affairs organization, the Council on Foreign Relations. He was a young man in his late twenties, who, through sheer grit and talent, had become part of the Eastern Establishment. In the eyes of CBS, Murrow's ability to sway domestic audiences might help this fledgling network educate its constituents about communications in the public interest, and in the process, win hearts and minds in Washington.

The 1934 Communications Act, which created the Federal Communications Commission, allowed networks to be set up as private entities only "if public convenience, interest or necessity will be served thereby," language first advanced in the Radio Act of 1927 when the federal government established control of the airwaves. CBS reacted in fear that if it did not bow to this government oversight with more public interest programming, it might not be able to continue to operate for profit as an entertainment medium. Murrow was hired in reaction to federal legislation that increased government regulation and oversight of programming. His meteoric rise at CBS could not be duplicated today.

The 1996 Telecommunications Act ended much of the federal regulation "bite" that came out of the early days of broadcast communications. Federal regulation today is bark without bite, as private, for-profit networks operate in a deregulated environment. There is no avenue in which public affairs programming like the Murrow vehicles *See It Now* or *CBS Reports* documentaries can thrive because broadcasters need only allow some spectrum for public affairs programming, but are not required by law to produce any quality public affairs programming themselves. Nicholas Lemann comments about the Murrow doctrine in *The New Yorker*: "CBS, in Murrow's heyday, felt that its prosperity, even its survival, depended on demonstrating to Washington its deep commitment to public affairs. The price of not doing so could be regulation, breakup, the loss of a part of the spectrum, or license revocation."[105] No such steep price remains today.

By the time Murrow transitioned out of the commercial broadcast medium, he brought with him to USIA twenty-five years of working largely for the public interest. His CBS salary of over $200,000 a year (what would translate into several million dollars today) wasn't typical of someone operating in the public interest, but the level of interest in his high quality programs warranted his steep compensation. Murrow proved the point for a quarter of the American 20th century: public affairs programs that address controversial social issues can be profitable to please the owners and shareholders at the top *and* also serve the public interest, which had a broader and more educational purpose that served the community and advanced civic understanding. The Murrow doctrine in journalism to this day means that public affairs programs need not be boring or noncontroversial, as commercial imperatives ventured toward the dramatic and sensational.

The two drives toward education and enlightenment on the one hand and entertainment and distraction on the other need not be in competition with each other with the latter winning out most of the time.

Murrow took this public interest philosophy to the United States Information Agency (USIA) in 1961. He was given the leadership mantle over an independent foreign affairs agency of 12,000 employees. He also had executive management over the Voice of America (VOA), the U.S.-Government sponsored international broadcasting service that delivered over 1,000 hours of programs to a global audience of 84 million in 55 languages. His deputy, former *Time* magazine editor and writer Donald M. Wilson, worked closely with Murrow and represented the director in many foreign policy crises when Murrow was too ill to be present. Wilson's "finest hour," according to Thomas Sorensen, was representing the Agency on the Executive Committee created in response to the Cuban missile crisis.[106] Murrow's finest hours are represented in the speeches that follow. This country owes Murrow a debt of gratitude for his many public addresses that served the domestic cause of the U.S. foreign policy process and purpose in the world. USIA's purpose under Murrow, "to operate on the basis of truth and make American policy at all times intelligible and, wherever possible, palatable to audiences abroad," took on a more weighty cause during the Kennedy years: to advise the president on current and future U.S. policies and programs, and to explain to foreign audiences important news stories in the United States, namely race-based stories that caught the attention of the world and which USIA was asked to put into proper context.

As late as July 1963, Murrow was explaining the challenges that his agency still had in communicating with the world:

> I would be derelict were I not to take notice that the effort to speak for the United States abroad has been short-changed. More money alone will not promise us success, but inadequate money may well threaten failure.

> We are a great power and are expected to render great leadership. We cannot expect miracles to flow from the folly of frugality.[107]

The low point for Murrow at USIA was his inability to get the Congressional funding he deemed necessary to maintain the Agency as a key player in policy formulation advice, explanation and promotion. This is why he accepted so many speaking engagements with American audiences. It was with these domestic constituents—the taxpayers—that he could make his strongest persuasive case.

Despite Murrow's up-and-down battles with Congress over appropriations, his USIA years were a highlight of his life. After retirement, he told Jean White at the Washington Post, "I have never worked harder in my life and never been happier. I haven't had such satisfaction since the days of covering the London blitz."[108]

When Kennedy died on November 22, 1963, it was said that part of Ed Murrow died along with the president whom he grew to respect.[109] When he officially departed USIA in January 1964, he was rich with offers from Hollywood to New York, from academe to private industry. But a year after he told Jean White he had "never been happier" and just eighteen months after he lost his president, Murrow too would be dead. Newspapers at the time were scarce in their commentary about his USIA years, those happiest years when Murrow served as America's chief propagandist. Perhaps they couldn't reconcile the journalist with the propagandist. But Murrow's "other hat" made propaganda work on behalf of the United States a respectable call to service. And in that service, despite a crippling illness, he felt a sense of satisfaction that transcended the celebrity mantle with which he was never comfortable. He had served a cause greater than himself.

Biographical sketch of Edward R. Murrow at the time of his nomination to be director of the United States Information Agency (Congressional Record, March 14, 1961):

Born: April 25, 1908, near Greensboro, N.C.

Education: Normal primary and secondary education in western Washington. Graduated Washington State College, 1930.
Marital status: Married.
Experience: 1930-32: President, National Student Federation (an organization of student body presidents). Traveled abroad during this period. 1932-33: Assistant Director, Institute of International Education, in charge of foreign offices, arranging student exchanges, publication of various pamphlets dealing with exchange professorships and equivalents of degrees between American and foreign universities. 1933-34: Assistant Secretary, Emergency Committee for Displaced German Scholars, an organization engaged in bringing German professors, dismissed by Hitler, to this country. 1935-37: Director of Talks and Education, Columbia Broadcasting System. 1937-46: European Director, CBS, London. Recruited and directed CBS news staff in Europe. 1946-48: Returned to New York as Vice President in charge of News and Public Affairs. 1948: Reporter, Director, and Producer, CBS. From that time until the present, engaged in production of radio and television news programs and documentaries, historical record albums and the editing of two books.
Honorary degrees: Brandeis University; Colby College; Grinnell College; Hamilton College; Mount Holyoke College; Muhlenburg College; University of North Carolina; Oberlin College; University of Rochester; Rollins College; Temple University; Washington State College.
Memberships: Board of trustees, Institute of International Education; Phi Beta Kappa; Kappa Sigma; Council on Foreign Relations.

Part Two

The Speeches of Edward R. Murrow

EDWARD R. MURROW
DIRECTOR
UNITED STATES INFORMATION AGENCY

1. Statement before the Committee on Foreign Relations, United States Senate, Washington, March 14, 1961
2. "Who Speaks for America?" National Press Club, Washington, May 24, 1961
3. Radio Television News Directors Association, Hotel Statler, Washington, September 30, 1961
4. Forum dinner with representatives of the Hollywood Film Industry, Los Angeles, November 5, 1961
5. The Lincoln Group of D.C., Willard Hotel, Washington, February 10, 1962
6. American Management Association, Annual Meeting, Palmer House Hilton, Chicago, February 16, 1962
7. National Association of Broadcasters, Shoreham Hotel, Washington, March 2, 1962
8. 59th Convention of the American Advertising Federation of America, Atlanta, GA, June 19, 1963
9. National Education Association, Detroit, Michigan, July 1, 1963
10. Federal Bar Association, Philadelphia, PA, September 26, 1963

1. Congressional Statement, March 14, 1961

Ye shall know the truth and the truth shall make you free.
John 8:32

When Edward R. Murrow appeared before the Committee on Foreign Relations on Tuesday, March 14, 1961, he was visibly nervous. It was not due to any shyness on his part. He was arguably the most famous political appointee in the Kennedy administration and his voice was recognized the world over. Murrow thought that he could not smoke inside the committee room. In fact, he could smoke, had he so chosen. But his enforced cessation from doing what he said he must do about every fifteen to thirty minutes of his waking time made it seem as if he were uncomfortable with the proceedings.

In his opening statement that follows, Murrow makes a pledge that is to this day associated with both his journalism and government service reputation: operate on the basis of truth. In journalism, such a pledge may be an easier commitment to make than for someone about to be confirmed the head of America's official propaganda agency. He also reaffirms a Murrow maxim about how an information agency should operate. Despite all the electronic communications of the day—the broadcasting efforts in radio, television and film, "the best form of communications is still face-to-face."

Throughout his three years as director of the United States Information Agency, this Murrow pledge of truth would remain a challenge. The U.S. government was fully engaged in a Cold War struggle "between the forces of freedom and those who would demean and brutalize mankind." It was a struggle for ideas and minds and truth alone—as in the facts—could not be solely deployed. While Murrow acknowledged that the United States shouldn't use the duplicitous tactics of dictatorships, it still must persuade global populations that the U.S. political system and ways of life were far superior to those of its ideological opponents, Communist Russia and its satellite countries and allies. This conviction was something he passionately shared with his boss, the 35th president of the United States.

John F. Kennedy and Edward R. Murrow were not personal friends. Murrow was suspicious and pessimistic by nature, a brooding, cerebral type who undoubtedly questioned the young senator's meteoric rise to the top of the American political establishment. Murrow viewed Kennedy's exalted position as the result of playing it safe and not making waves as the junior senator from Massachusetts. Unlike Murrow, Kennedy did not take on America's dirty laundry—McCarthyism or its treatment of the lowly migrant worker who picked produce under the watchful eyes of the crew chief. John F. Kennedy was also the son of the appeaser Joseph P. Kennedy, who had resigned as U.S. Ambassador to Britain in October 1940, London's darkest hour. Murrow in contrast stood firmly in favor of American intervention and let it be known early on in his broadcasts. Murrow admired men who stood alone and took great risks on principle. He saw neither the father nor the son as such a man. Joseph Kennedy was a businessman first and a politician second, who saw wars as interruptions to commerce, while John Kennedy was born into privilege and learned to work the system to his favor.

Despite this past, Ed Murrow and John Kennedy remained distant admirers of each other's American liberal roots, public service, and professional accomplishments. Kennedy's stock from a privileged Irish Catholic heritage in Boston mandated a noblesse oblige to the less fortunate and a call to the highest level of public service from the family patriarch. Murrow came from much more humble Quaker stock in North Carolina where he was reared on the rhythmic cadences of the King James Bible. Born in a 1750s farmhouse on Polecat Creek, Murrow grew into a man of promise in the Pacific Northwest where he delighted in hard manual labor as he honed his public speaking skills at Washington State. In short order, Murrow was traveling social and intellectual circles in New York as elite and influential as those Kennedy had known since birth.

Both men saw war up close and personal, Kennedy in the Pacific and Murrow as a war correspondent in Europe. Both were born before America's entry into World War I, the war, like so many before and since, that would "end all wars." Influenced by two world wars and a third cold war, they could speak the language of American promise in the face of peril.

These two men who were not friends needed each other as friends do: the fearless American commentator to build bona fide credentials with the liberal establishment and a New Frontiersman to rebuild the former journalist's self-worth. By 1960, each was an A-list celebrity in his own right. Murrow, who at one time could name his price in broadcast journalism, had been searching for an out from CBS. He was all but through with television and felt a strong need to serve his country again as he felt he had served it while stationed in Europe. Kennedy's election in November 1960 was his out from CBS and a possible opening with Washington. His wife Janet would later call the Kennedy offer a "brilliant and timely gift."[110]

Kennedy, the younger to Murrow by nine years, knew he had a formidable nominee in Murrow, who, if never admired by conservatives, was seen as the gold standard in American journalism. The Murrow tradition in journalism was to set an example for those who aspired to be the best of the press, to imbue the profession with dignity and an ever-vigilant search for truth, even if the truth might hurt. Murrow's reputation for helping to bring down Joe McCarthy buoyed Kennedy's reputation with his liberal core constituents who questioned the new president's rather milquetoast response to McCarthyism in the 1950s. With Murrow, Kennedy had a chance to raise his own administration's prestige along with America's prestige in the world. Murrow's crusading against totalitarian thinking at home would also transfer well in the ideological crusade against Communist totalitarianism.

Murrow's executive appointment was announced in late January 1961 and six weeks later Murrow sat before Congress to share his architectural plans for how he would rebuild America's official persuasive framework. The experience was one that likely made him squirm. Like his former boss William Paley at CBS, Murrow did not take kindly to too much personal scrutiny by members of Congress. A man whose entire career was on one side of the microphone doing commentary on the most important events of his day now had to reveal more of his own philosophy as the microphone was pointed at him. As a journalist, he could allow the facts of the story to lead without too much political editorializing. At USIA, the facts would continue to lead, but as a government bureaucrat they would unfold in a persuasive political milieu, both domestic and foreign. And unlike in his former broadcast haunts where Murrow was held in godlike admiration, in the halls of Congress he would face members who did not fawn over his every word, much less his appeals for funding. He was, after all, the head of the U.S. Information Agency, which had been a political football since its founding nearly a decade before.

On that Tuesday in March, U.S. Senator Henry M. Jackson of Washington introduced his fellow resident to the Senate Committee on Foreign Relations chaired by Arkansas Democrat Senator J. William Fulbright. Other majority members present included Senators Hubert Humphrey (D-MN), Frank Church (D-ID), and Mike Mansfield (D-MT), along with minority members George Aiken (R-VT), Bourke Hickenlooper (R-IA), and Homer Capehart (R-IN).

Senator Jackson's opening remarks emphasized the great personal sacrifice Murrow undertook to leave the private sector for the public sector. "I think Mr. Murrow sets an example for the kind of men that we need in the Government during these trying and dangerous times."

Those trying and dangerous times were plenty, both at home and overseas. Reverend Martin Luther King, Jr., had six months earlier been arrested trying to integrate a lunch counter in Atlanta. The Eisenhower administration had begun an embargo against Communist Cuba that banned all commodities with the exception of medical supplies and a few food products. The public, much less Murrow, had no knowledge of a military intervention against Cuba that was just weeks away and that would set the stage for a much greater role for USIA and Murrow in particular.

In March 1961, the Soviet Union's battle for hearts and minds in the Third World was by far the biggest threat against the United States and shaped all the rhetoric emerging from the United States Information Agency. This was a contest: a battle of wills, way of life, and values.

Murrow told the Congress that there is no time limit or set price on such a contest and the United States had no guarantee of winning. It must try, however, and not by threatening, but through persuasion. Persuasion is what Murrow had been using his whole life to tell stories at a commercial network. Now he had to persuade many audiences: Congress, his staff, the American people, global publics, Kennedy's cabinet. Chairman Fulbright instructed, "Well I am sure you know, Mr. Murrow, that the USIA has been somewhat controversial in its relation to the Congress?" Murrow's reply: "Yes, sir."

After this first grilling at the hands of Congress, Murrow told writer David Halberstam that though he had watched many Congressional hearings and felt that he knew what to expect, he encountered something entirely new. "The essential change is this: You sit there and have in a sense, your integrity as a reporter questioned. And yet you don't have the freedom in answering and maneuvering you would have as an individual or you might want because you are responsible for an agency and its appropriations and you always have to keep this in mind, your responsibility to others."[111]

Edward R. Murrow
Nomination to be Director
United States Information Agency
Washington, D.C.
March 14, 1961

Senator Henry M. Jackson from the State of Washington: Mr. Chairman, this is really a three-State presentation. The nominee was born in North Carolina; he grew up in the State of Washington; and he has a home in New York.

One of the real problems we face in the cold war is to bring to Government men of the caliber of Mr. Murrow. Studies that have been made to find how we can do a better job in this area of great challenge, always point the finger to the competency of appointees. We have been conducting some studies of this problem and have just released a report yesterday on the private citizen and the national service.

In my judgment, Mr. Murrow brings to this important agency a high degree of competency and courage. He is a man with a very keen intellect.

He comes to this office at a great personal sacrifice. It is difficult to get qualified men to leave industry and leave business to serve their country. I think Mr. Murrow sets an example for the kind of men that we need in the Government during these trying and dangerous times. I am confident that he will render great service to his country, as he has in the past in the private sector dealing with the problems of public affairs.

Mr. Murrow: My name is Edward R. Murrow. I was christened Egbert but abandoned that name at the age of 16 while working in the logging camps in western Washington.

Most of my adult life has been spent in the periphery of the academic world and in the field of radio and television. These activities have involved considerable travel, at home and abroad, and some acquaintance with statesmen, educators, and newsmen in many countries.

As a foreign correspondent, I am more familiar with the work of the United States Information Agency abroad than here in Washington.

At the conclusion of a trip around the world several months ago, I gave it as my opinion that the work of USIA abroad had improved very considerably under the direction of Ambassador George Allen, and am pleased to have the opportunity to repeat that opinion here.

If I am confirmed in the office to which the President has nominated me, I shall attempt to discharge the duties and responsibilities of the office to the best of my ability.

The Agency will attempt to make U.S. policy, as designed by the President, everywhere intelligible and wherever possible, palatable.

We shall endeavor to reflect with fidelity to our allies, to the uncommitted nations, and to those who are hostile to us, not only our policy but our ideals.

We shall operate on the basis of truth. Being convinced that we are engaged in hot and implacable competition with Communist forces around the world, we will not be content to counter their lies and distortions. We shall constantly reiterate our faith in freedom.

To the emerging nations we shall say, "We share your dreams." There is a dynamism in freedom which permits and encourages progress without binding the individual to the wheel of the state. We shall try to make it clear that we as a Nation are not allergic to change and have no desire to sanctify the status quo. This Nation not only has a birth certificate, it holds the patent rights on change and revolution by consent.

The Agency will try to speak on behalf of all the American people with restraint and reason. All of us in the Agency recognize that in spite of electronic developments, the best form of communications is still face-to-face. To that end, any men and women we recruit and train must be able and eager to serve the cause of freedom which we regard as being indivisible.

The voice of this country should at all times be steady—firm but not bellicose—carrying the conviction that we will not flinch or falter in the face of threats or provocations.

In the end of the day it may well be that the example of this Nation will be more important than its dollars or its words. If we, in this generous and capacious land, can demonstrate increasing equality of opportunity, social justice, a reasoned concern for the education, health and the equality under law of all our citizens, we will powerfully affect, and probably determine, the destiny of the free world and that freedom may be contagious, may incite those who have lost that most precious of all possessions to strive to do likewise.

No man can set either a time or dollar limit upon this contest between the forces of freedom and those who would demean and brutalize mankind. The contest will be prolonged and it will cost much treasure. There is not guarantee that we will win it. If we should lose, it will be by default, and history will take its revenge. We cannot imitate the tactics or the techniques of the dictatorships that now ride the backs of most of this planet's people. We cannot threaten, we must persuade. Freedom cannot be imposed, it must be sought for, and frequently fought for.

We live a world we didn't make. We are honored by an awesome responsibility of leadership we did not seek. We must defend and expand the leadership in company with our allies and other like-minded peoples because that is what our history and our heritage demand of us. We are the pivot upon which the history of our time must turn. Our task is formidable and difficult, but difficulty is one excuse history has never accepted.

We must, I think, approach the task with patience and fortitude and with an abiding belief that not only our own ancestors who bought our freedom for us but all those who have suffered and struggled and died in the pursuit of freedom throughout all time are watching to see whether we be worthy of our heritage.

If I am confirmed in the office to which the President has appointed me, I will, together with my colleagues in the Agency, attempt to be worthy of the trust.

2. National Press Club, May 24, 1961

I love America more than any other country in this world, and, exactly for this reason, I insist on the right to criticize her perpetually. James Baldwin

John P. Cosgrove was president of the National Press Club in 1961, an auspicious time for anyone serving in that capacity given the change in administration. The 40-something Kennedy had replaced the septuagenarian Eisenhower. It was a happy time in Washington, according to Cosgrove, who celebrates his 95th birthday in 2013. (Were he still alive today, JFK would have turned 96 on May 29, 2013.)

The National Press Club pattern then was to write to speakers in advance when they were in the news or about to make news. Obviously new cabinet officers and new faces in the Kennedy administration were of interest to the NPC as newsmakers and were sent formal invitations to speak. Arthur Goldberg, Secretary of Labor, who would later be appointed Associate Justice of the U.S. Supreme Court, was one of the first speakers. Cosgrove didn't hear back from the new director of the United States Information Agency, though he assumed Murrow would be one of the first Kennedy appointees to accept the invitation to speak to his former peers.

Cosgrove bumped into Murrow at the White House Correspondents' Association Dinner in February and once again pressed Mr. Murrow to come speak at the National Press Club. Mr. Murrow said he had received the invitation but still hadn't decided to go. His experience thus far in Washington was far different than Murrow had envisioned. Murrow told Cosgrove, "I don't know if I'm going to fit in with the government way of doing things." Cosgrove responded, "Well, that's news. Come and tell why, what the problem is. Maybe this can do some good and ease the way for private people to come into the public sector government service." Murrow said he would think about it and invited Cosgrove to have a drink at the Wardman Park Hotel where they could talk about it some more.

In the Metronome Room at the hotel, the waiters recognized Murrow and were glad to have him at their watering hole. It was late and the lounge was about to close, but the waiters offered a last call drink and said that the two men could stay and carry on with their conversation. When they were ready to leave, all they had to do was to close the door behind them. Such was the influence a man like Murrow had in 1960s Washington.

What Murrow shared with Cosgrove that long night into the wee hours was how difficult government service could be. You have that board of directors across town, those 535 on Capitol Hill who want to know everything you are doing. You can't do "a damn thing" without getting the money from them. Murrow never liked to go hat in hand to plead his cause, whether it was to the suits at CBS or the suits on the Hill. Congressional oversight and control of the money coffers was part of what bothered Mr. Murrow about Washington.

When he finally accepted the invitation to speak at the National Press Club for late May 1961, Murrow had spent time reflecting on the talented staff he had at USIA. It was a different breed of cat than what he was used to working with at CBS, but the government bureaucrats he supervised were doing a good job and he was glad to be associated with them. Yes, he had to accept that he must go to the Hill to plead the fiscal case for his agency, but it wasn't as bad as originally thought. He would let the good tidings of USIA be known to the public through this National Press Club speech and the many others to follow. He would fill the prescription for change that Kennedy had advocated at his inaugural. Murrow would do for his country in his senior years as he had done for his private commercial employer in his youth and middle age.

John Cosgrove's perspective on Murrow is that despite being the senior statesman of the Kennedy circle, Murrow had the spirit of the Peace Corps youth who answered Kennedy's call in 1961. Just as Murrow had been brought out of retirement from CBS for public service, the Peace Corps brought young people straight out of the university or who were yet to enroll at university. These were not the "ugly Americans" of Burdick and Lederer fame. The Peace Corps volunteers were living like the native peoples to whom they were assigned. And Murrow, in his way, was doing a similar thing in bringing his talents to USIA, living the life of the native government bureaucrats whom he came to appreciate and admire for helping him maneuver the Washington political milieu. Like those youth, Murrow saw his role as that of a democratic propagandist for good—he could tell America's story to the world just as the Peace Corps volunteers were living the story overseas.

Murrow's talk at the Press Club was the first USIA speech I selected for this book. It's easy to see why. Murrow is funny, open with his compatriot press brothers and sisters, and hopeful that as head of the United States Information Agency he will be able to effectively communicate America's official story to the world. He is still enjoying his prolonged honeymoon with Washington as the most famous face of the administration outside the executive office, and the board of directors, aka Congressional appropriations committee overseeing USIA funding, has not yet left a permanent burn mark upon his psyche. That would come later. He feels at one with the capacity crowd of 490, what at the time was one of the largest luncheon speaker gatherings of any National Press Club event.

A very extensive question-and-answer period follows Murrow's formal remarks and in this period Murrow is characteristically frank, though leavened with humor. Cosgrove reads one of the questions:

> **Cosgrove:** Is it true that you are resigning from USIA because you were not consulted in the Cuban fiasco?
>
> **Murrow:** Mr. President, this story that I am resigning was obviously the result of free journalistic enterprise. (Audience laughter) I have never spoken of resigning. I have never thought of resigning. I have not even had any dreams about resigning. (Laughter) I am happy in my work...the rations are adequate. I am in goodly company and, at least until I made this speech here

today, Mr. President, I was not aware that I was in any danger of being fired. (Audience laughter and applause)

The speech is to be celebrated for Murrow's ability to connect headlines of the day in the U.S., bus bombings of freedom riders in Alabama, with the struggle for freedom around the world. America's domestic struggles are "absorbed, debated, and pondered on all shores of every ocean." He also relates how difficult it is at times for diplomatic representatives from African nations to find good housing in Washington, a reality that the Communists don't have to propagate. "We do it ourselves in our own capital."

Edward R. Murrow
Who Speaks for America?
National Press Club
Washington, D.C.
May 24, 1961

Introduction of Murrow by Club President John P. Cosgrove

Gentlemen, while you are finishing your desert and last sip of coffee, I thought we would start the proceedings. As you might know, our guest today has been a frontiersman long before any of his fellow New Frontiersmen. And he is a man of many talents. He's taught more than almost anybody in the world. And now he is attempting to acquire anonymity. He calls himself the Satchel Paige of the Kennedy Administration. And he's been compared to Joan of Arc, not altogether because of the voice situation, but as someone said, because he's smoking more now and enjoying it less.

Edward R. Murrow has won just about every honor, citation, plaque, and award that can be given to a broadcast journalist. He also has at least thirteen honorary degrees, plus honorary titles from Great Britain, France and Belgium. All of this was accomplished during his almost twenty-five years with CBS. Remember those early years when he reported the turbulent 30s from Europe, the Nazi invasion of Austria. Later, "This is London" broadcasts and then came peace and television and programs which are household words today: Small World, Person to Person, CBS Reports, See It Now. All are strongly identified with our speaker today. He was born in Greensboro, North Carolina in 1908 and his family moved to the state of Washington in 1920 where he worked in logging camps. This was his first touch of the New Frontier or at least the frontier. Later he graduated from the Washington State College with honors, Phi Beta Kappa, as you probably know. From 1930 to 1932, he was president of the National Student Federation. And then he joined what might be compared today to the Peace Corps, the Institute of International Education, which is financed by the way by the Carnegie and Rockefeller Foundations. And as an Assistant Director of that institute, from 1932 to 1935, he served as head of its offices in London, Paris, Berlin, Geneva, and Vienna. And reflecting back to that, Ed Murrow says, "We raised a million and a half dollars to bring out ninety of the best minds from Germany. It was the most satisfying thing I ever did in my life." CBS, taking note of this experience and background, named him Director of its European Affairs in 1937. I think he had been on the scene about two years before he became Director of its European Operations. The next few years, particularly those in London, will be relived during the immediate years ahead at the USIA. And perhaps will serve to revitalize and reinforce his fortitude and stamina. Twice bombs fell on Columbia's London offices as Murrow was broadcasting. A New York superior remarked, "He sticks to his posts, for he is an almost uncontrollable daredevil." Later he was positively forbidden to take a cruise on a Minesweeper. He did it anyway and broadcast a description of his experiences. During the Blitz of London, he spent night after night atop BBC's broadcasting house practicing ad lib descriptions of the flaming raids. He wanted to broadcast an eyewitness account, but the censors refused, for fear his words heard in Berlin might be shortwaved back to the high-flying Nazi planes. So he practiced descriptions which would give nothing away, and finally won permission to make an ad-lib broadcast. That's another experience that I'm sure will stand by him in his years ahead. I say years ahead, advisedly. For this and other outstanding service, CBS made him Vice President and Director of Public Affairs in 1946, but he returned as a newscaster a year later. He signed off as VP with these haunting words: "I'm not an executive. Budgets, in-baskets and out-baskets are not for me." Recently he said, and I don't know if he was commenting on that statement or not, but he said, "I was never one to contend that I was always right."

Now after a quarter of a century in a field where he attained more honors and accolades than any one person, he moves into an area which shall provide him with the maximum opportunity to receive more brickbats and see more horrors than any one person. He has changed hats, shifted gears, and moved back to the executive suite. The transition, of course, will not be easy. First, there's a 90% cut in salary. Ask not what you can give to your country. (Laughter and smattering applause) Then he must adjust himself to look at the government from the inside instead of from the outside looking in. He's also working harder, he says, harder than he's ever worked before. Gentlemen, this is the man that William S. Paley, the top man at CBS, described as follows in 1941: "He's a man fitted to his time and to his task: a student, a philosopher, at heart a poet of mankind. And therefore a great reporter." It is my pleasure now to present to you the new and still director of the USIA (More laughter), Edward R. Murrow.

Edward R. Murrow

Mr. President and fellow workers, including those who work in the wasteland, since Washington is a city where rumors ripen even in inclement weather, I should perhaps begin by denying one. There is no truth whatever Mr. President, in the contention that I came to Washington because I discovered that a new television show program was underway, which was to star a horse, a talking horse with a fine stable of writers, and he was to be called Mr. Ed. I was not concerned lest my image be blurred by that new program.

This is the first time I have attempted to raise my voice in public. I have been trying to learn my lesson, seeking a bit of that anonymity that many people believe I so richly deserve. You have done me great honor in asking me here, and beggar that I am, I am even poorer in thanks. But I must confess that it is with mingled pleasure and awe that I join you today, pleasure at being again among so many of my former colleagues, awe that I am now the object of those scowling, critical visages, among whose array I once sat with my own frowning brow. The frowning brow has not changed. We have only changed seats, and I must now answer questions instead of propounding them.

I have been in my job as Director of the Agency scant weeks. Operating as we do in 98 countries around the world, there is much about the Agency that I have yet to learn. But as a former working newsman like most of you here today, there are a number of thoughts and impressions that I would share with you in my present unfamiliar role as a government official.

Our Agency operates in a difficult, not too well defined area. We embrace a multitude of disciplines and professions. Many of you are newsmen who devote your careers, as I did for 25 years, to expression in a single medium of communication. USIA employs not one, but seven: radio, television, movies, press, book publishing, exhibits and the arts. We are involved in an entire range of technical problems.

Even more important, we must deal also amidst the intangibles: the difficult, delicate human art of persuasion. For by word of mouth, by cultivated personal contact abroad, we seek to persuade others of the rightness of our view and that our actions and goals are in harmony with theirs. And this brings on a thought: in the course of a single working day how many of you gentlemen here could exercise your expertise competently over an array of problems as diverse as these?

To those bold enough to reply in the affirmative, I offer a note of caution: this is only half of the Agency's problem. For we deal not only in communications but also in policy. We articulate and distribute not advertising for cigarettes and soapsuds but clarifications of government policy and deeds. And we speak in many languages to many peoples of vastly differing cultures and styles, of vastly differing levels of comprehension. We must deal also with the very considerable pre-conditioning foreigners have had to the image and the ideas of America. We must deal with the realities of their fears, their concerns, their stereotypes—however unjustified, their existence is nevertheless real—of the product we promote: the actions and the hopes of the United States.

Thus the effective overseas USIA officer must be a creature who combines the talents of professional proficiency with persistence and patience. He must try to know as much about seven media of communication as most of you gentlemen know about your one. I shall not indulge your sufferance by reading a list of the qualifications of the officers in the Agency. But I assure you that I have found that I'm able to call upon resourceful minds of many disciplines. We have men who number among their accomplishments before coming with the Agency such positions as a broadcast Peabody Award winner; a past President of NBC International; a former producer with Eagle Lion and Warner Brothers studio; the former President of a college; several deans of universities, including a Dean Emeritus from Columbia University; an original editor of Newsweek; an author of 15 published novels, 6 of which have been adapted for motion pictures; editors of metropolitan newspapers and national press services; overseas bureau chiefs, foreign correspondents and Nieman fellows in journalism.

In my first four months, I have asked many of my colleagues to postpone fellowships, assignments abroad and desirable posts long anticipated. Often at great personal inconvenience, their invariable response has been: "Whatever you think is best for the Agency, I will gladly do."

So it was that one of my long-held illusions about government was somewhat shattered when I assumed this office. For my own part, as your president has remarked, I have never worked harder in my life or enjoyed it more. I have never been called a loafing man, though on occasion I confess a certain predilection for good conversation, good wine and decent food, but not since the days of World War II have I worked with what I suppose could be called such a frantic fascination.

I am finding that, in my experience at least, this is truly a time of the "New Zeal," and it is not easy to set the pace for my younger colleagues. As you have been told and the quote was accurate, I feel at times like the Satchel Paige of this administration. Our work product would stagger the mind of what we in government call "private enterprise." Our radio broadcasts live over 88 hours a day in 35 languages. Our special wireless file puts out 8-10,000 words a day to each of five world areas. Our films reach an estimated weekly audience of about 150 million people. And in television our "market" is rapidly expanding: 36 million TV sets and 160 million viewers.

Nor is our product dissipated meaninglessly. For the 50 million books we have published in 50 languages, there is incessant demand. In Nyasaland a library opened in March of this year, and the borrowers stripped the shelves bare of the 1,500 volumes in less than a month of operation. In another post in Africa, there was a greater demand for the Federalist Papers recorded in a period of four weeks than was recorded in the New York Public Library in the course of an entire year. And the first English classes formed in two newly independent countries numbered among their pupils both Prime Ministers, a number of Cabinet officials, as well as other high government leaders and their wives.

Our Agency, as you know by Congressional mandate, operates overseas. There is much misunderstanding about just what the U.S. Information Agency does. We have received letters with certain ominous overtones such as request to "send all information you have on counterfeiting" and "please rush me all the facts on bullet wounds—and fast." I shall keep a copy of the reply to that, Mr. President. Letter writers have asked just "what percentage of young people are juveniles, how can I figure out which TV newscasters are Republican."

Information is our job but information of more serious import.

We shall endeavor to reflect with fidelity to our allies, to the uncommitted nations, as well as to those who are hostile to us, not only our policy but our ideals. Yet in our
day-to-day efforts directed to this end, we do not stand alone. For much that is known and believed about this country is beyond the purview of our Agency alone.

Just as the work of USIA is far more than just the Voice of America broadcast, so is the real voice of America far, far more than just our Agency. From Norway to Nyasaland, from Rio to Rangoon, the story and the face of America goes out in movies, television, magazines, and the press. The military, with fighters and their families, number one million abroad. Over four million American tourists travel abroad each year. Another half million Americans live overseas for reasons embracing both business and pleasure. Foundations, educational exchanges, and international scholarships send our young intellectuals and their studious professors swarming to foreign universities. Fifty thousand foreign students and hundreds of thousands of foreign tourists will visit our country every year to hear and evaluate the first-hand voice of America.

And all of this has great impact. Italy has built its first drive-in movie. An authentic drugstore stands in the shadow of the Arc de Triomphe. England, God bless its warm draft lager, is beginning to drink cold beer in cans, and I do not evaluate the effect of that. Even Moscow has succumbed, not only to jazz and Louis Armstrong, but also, and heaven assuage the souls of Marx and Lenin, to American installment buying. And these are but the frothy facts of the spreading style of America or the 20th Century, since both in so many ways are synonymous.

Beneath them, and of far more lasting impact, is the broadening outward flow of ideas and techniques of how to live and work together, of respect for neighbors, of faith that every human problem is capable of human solution. We and all the other voices of America that reach outside our frontiers are helping to spread the concept of "access," of individual self-fulfillment, and citizen participation—the impression that democracy's business is never done.

I tell you all this not to defend our culture but to define our Agency. You gentlemen of the press share very much with our Agency the making of the picture of America that is known abroad.

And the impact made on these people through the press is of course largely beyond the influence of the USIA. Yet the picture is even broader. Not only the press, but television, the movies, the traveling tourists, the missionaries, and the businessmen, are part of the chorus that is the real voice of America.

To some of us the picture of a burning bus in Alabama may merely represent the speed, the initiative, and the competence of a good photographer, but to those of us in the U.S. Information Agency it means that picture will be front-paged tomorrow all the way from Manila to Rabat. Here in Washington itself, for example, there exists a much unreported encumbrance on our African relations that can lose us as much influence as anything the Soviet Union might do. Where do we house our African diplomats in this capital? It is of course bad enough that they read headlines of Birmingham bus burnings and beatings. It is even worse that they find it near impossible to live in the capital of our nation. Landlords will not rent to them; schools refuse their children; stores will not let them try on clothes; beaches ban their families. Today there are some 30 African representatives in Washington without what is euphemistically called "satisfactory housing." Fully one-third of these are termed emergency cases. There will be some 50 more families arriving in the next six months, 100 in the next year. It is not only that these people are humans like the rest of us, but that they are leaders of their nations whose friendship this land deems vital. We would have them join our company of honorable men in defending against encroachment our dedication to dignity and freedom. But it is a dignity to which we will not fully admit them.

And if there should be dire repercussions, it would be recounted as a diplomatic debacle for the United States. And if and when that day should come, do not fly to your Information Agency crying that we have not told "our story" abroad. For in this damaging indignity there is blame enough for us all. And let us remember, this is not something the Communists did to us. We do it ourselves in our own capital. Is it possible that we concern ourselves too much with outer space and far places, and too little with inner space and near places?

Let me turn back to the subject at hand. You did not invite me here to talk about our duty and our opportunity as citizens, rather to tell you about our work. Quite reasonably, you wish to know where we hope to go and how we shall try to get there. At the outset let me emphasize that I did not bring to the Agency the infinite wisdom of an outsider with magic cures for all that's wrong. I have discovered that almost everyone knows how this Agency should be run except myself.

In fact, much of what I have found is good, effective, and solid. I recognize, as I know you will too, that the role of our Agency has limits. We are but one arm of the U.S. government. As such, we must respond to the policy of that government. To put it more bluntly, USIA can be no better than the policies it supports and explains. Yet within that limitation there are obviously practices and principles to which we are committed. It is fundamental that we operate on the basis of truth. Ours is, and must be, a dedication to the factual.

But this itself poses difficulties. We operate abroad; our audience is foreign. Candor and openness have their merits as the successful Alan Shepherd demonstrated. They also have their demerits as the abortive Cuban episode demonstrated.

On Cuba, we had no choice but to be truthful and complete. At noon on April 17, we expanded our Spanish broadcasting to Latin America from one hour of origination to 19 hours. Within two hours we were on the air. I mention this with some degree of pride. What network could undertake such expansion on such short notice with no change in the personnel allowance?

There were Latins relaying our broadcasts who said, "you are too honest, you will be misunderstood." There were Americans who protested, as the letter writer from California who heard the tirades of Dr. Paul Roa on our Spanish broadcasts and suggested we leave such broadcasting to the Voice of Castro. The answer was that Dr. Roa was speaking in the United Nations debate, which we carried in its entirety. We carried the whole story—Castro's announcement, the self-labeled "invasion," the writhing in Washington, the agonies in the UN, and even the agonizing reappraisal, which a critical aftermath spilled over the Administration.

But if truth must be our guide then dreams must be our goal. To the hunger of those masses yearning to be free and to learn, to this sleeping giant now stirring, that is so much of the world, we shall say: "We share your dreams." As a nation, we have never been allergic to change. Ours was the first of the great revolutions. It is a birthright we do not intend to let go by default. Our responsibilities of nationhood are predicated on a helping hand to others who would elevate their crushing way of existence by change into a more bountiful society. We offer no panaceas, no final solutions. We offer to join in the search for betterment. We offer our experience and our energies in partnership in the quest for greater human excellence. This we not only endorse. This we sponsor and promote, and indeed, provoke. A tradition of government by the governed, of revolution by consent—all of these are among the greater virtues that we have to demonstrate to a world that is sorely in need of great virtues.

How shall we accomplish these goals?

First, the projects that we launch are delivered abroad primarily through our posts. Those posts and their relation to Washington represent the rim of a wheel to a hub. We in Washington set policy and direction for our posts abroad, but it is as a service center to our overseas operators that we serve our main function.

I have already mentioned that we operate in seven principal media of communication: radio, television, movies, press, book publishing, exhibits and the arts. As the informational arm of US policy, what we do is often imposed on us by the impact of events. But we do not await events. We anticipate and try to prepare and organize our resources.

We are concentrating our attention on the fields where the ideological competition is being waged. This means expansion in Africa—where new nations have arisen—and in Latin America—where new difficulties have been born—and in Southeast Asia—where new pressures are upon us. We will not do this, however, at the expense of thinning the lines of communication with our traditional friends and allies.

But we shall try to do more than merely affirm the negative. We shall examine and explain the promise of the new "Alliance for Progress," the economic and social promise that can bloom from the new planted seedling of US-Latin American cooperation.

In Africa, there are new lands emerging with new leaders. It is a continent groping for directions, churning with ideas, surveying our style, sampling our ideals, looking about in search of new allegiances. One need only recall the heady wine of our own independence in 1776 to appreciate the new intoxication of Africa. And to them we must do more than criticize their politics and caution them about the Soviet Union. We must share with them our hands and our hearts, our techniques and our time. And we must, perhaps above all, accord them the dignity of friendship and respect.

In Southeast Asia we are taking additional urgent steps to communicate our determination to support our allies and to prevent neutral countries from falling to Communism. Communication in these lands is poor. Literacy is low. The challenge to our ingenuity and to our energy is great and it is expensive.

Our financing this year will, we hope, be adequate. But I would remind you that our budget now awaiting approval was drawn up before the sudden increase in the menace of Castro's Communism, before the stepped up Communist assault in Laos and the eroding subversion in South Vietnam and Thailand.

In the matter of financial and manpower substance, our adversaries have a clear advantage. The Soviet bloc spends more money jamming our radio broadcasts than we spend on our entire Agency. Our total budget is less than the cost of one combat-loaded Polaris submarine, and it is one-fifth of the estimated advertising budget of our armaments manufacturers. One American soap company spends almost as much on advertising as the USIA spends explaining United States policy abroad.

We certainly do not solicit billions for propagating the truth. But this country must be willing to do what must be done or we will forfeit to the inexorable tide of history our role as the promoters of freedom.

Implicit in meeting this challenge is the cost of physical facility. The Voice of America broadcasts 600 hours a week and, including packaged programs, uses up to 62 languages. But as they say in the trade, let's look at the competition. We are fourth, ranked in order behind Russia, Communist China, and the United Arab Republic. But we certainly do not intend to remain in fourth position. We are building new transmitters, one in North Carolina, one in Liberia, but we are seriously handicapped against the opposition because they are already located physically closer to much of the audience we would reach. We have had practically no increase in transmitter power since 1953 and it was in these years that our competition passed us.

Our broadcast and other activities do need more money, but money alone will not do the job. We need immunization from accordion financing, granting most of our budget requests one year and squeezing them tightly the next. No network or newspaper could flourish on such financial irregularity; neither can the USIA.

We face a difficult time with staffing. We need more permanent staff, talented people to work for little pay and less recognition. And we need the cooperation of the men who help shape the thinking of our citizens. We want them to share their thoughts abroad. In Moscow and Peiping, such intellectuals and journalists are summoned at government bidding. In America, we do not bid; we request. We need your help and we cannot pay commercial rates. But we can offer another compensation—the satisfaction that you helped keep your country strong.

The history of this Agency has been brief and turbulent. I trust its future will be long and fruitful. In the bare 20 years of its life, it has had five titles and twelve directors. The casualty rate, Mr. President, has been high.

The product of this Agency is all for export, much of it invisible, much of it unknown at home. Much of its end product is not measurable by common standards. We do not have a rating service, and frequently our work is known to the public only when we make a mistake. We do not ask you gentlemen for special consideration and certainly not for sympathy.

We do not ask that our mistakes be ignored, nor that our accomplishments be exaggerated. We shall do our best to tell you what the Agency is doing in the belief that you are as concerned as we in providing the citizens of this country with information as to what is being said and done in their name abroad.

I have learned since coming to Washington at least two things: the first is that it is much easier to ask questions than to answer them, and the second, that questions are never indiscreet but answers sometimes are. I would suppose that the art of answering is to produce a proper mixture of candor and discretion and to confess ignorance when that ignorance is obvious. That I shall try to do, Mr. President.

Questions and Answers at Edward R. Murrow's Speech before the National Press Club, Washington, D.C., May 24, 1961

Q: First question, as America's Vice President in charge of international public relations, are you habitually consulted before the fat is in the fire?

A: I suppose the obvious answer to that is to ask for a definition of both the fat and the fire, since there seems to be no shortage of either. I would answer it, however, by saying that it was suggested when I came down here that this Agency could operate effectively only if it had (1) prior access to information; (2) an opportunity to be heard on policy before policy was made. I have no complaints on that score. At the same time, I have no illusions that I am monopolizing the making of policy. (Audience laughter) But I do—I do have an opportunity to be heard.

Q: Is it true that you are resigning from USIA because you were not consulted in the Cuban fiasco?

A: Mr. President, this story that I am resigning was obviously the result of free journalistic enterprise. (Audience laughter) I have never spoken of resigning. I have never thought of resigning. I have not even had any dreams about resigning. (Laughter) I am happy in my work…the rations are adequate. I am in goodly company and, at least until I made this speech here today, Mr. President, I was not aware that I was in any danger of being fired. (Audience laughter and applause)

Mr. John Cosgrove, President of the National Press Club, who acted as master of ceremonies interpolated: There is one thing, Ed, things break fast in Washington, however. (More laughter)

Q: What do you say to reports that you are irked over lack of information given you by the White House, State Department and CIA?

A: Irked is not the word. Obviously, I am not able to contribute details as to the degree and frequency of consultation, but inside this room I was somewhat irked when after a considerable session with the President on Monday, he had me on the telephone at 8:30 the following morning before I had got to my office. I can only repeat that I have no complaints on the degree or the frequency of consultation. I would not care to rack up a box score as to how many I have won or lost, but the opportunity to go to bat exists.

Q: Could you please explain your statement that USIA was "truthful and complete" about the Cuban invasion, in view of the fact that the US Government at the time professed to know nothing about it and even now has not described its role in it on the record?

A: By "truthful and complete" I meant to say that we reported such evidence, such events, as were available. That we quoted the American press, the American wire agencies. We quoted foreign reaction. That we delivered the complete and absolute final historical version, one that will be accepted by history, obviously we didn't. I don't think any of us did. What I meant by that statement was that we did a full, straightaway job of reporting.

Q: How do you put a favorable light for the rest of the world on such news as the current race disturbances in Alabama?

A: The answer is that you don't. They happened. They are fully reported. For a period of two days, the difficulties in Alabama led most of the European broadcast news bulletin and led the papers. They also led the Voice of America broadcasts. The thing that we did do was (1) to report what happened, with, I hope, brevity and clarity, and also to put the emphasis on the speed and effectiveness of the action taken first by the Federal Government and then by the State authorities to restore order. Beyond that we could not go, and should not.

Q: Shifting gears here again, to meet the problem of housing African diplomats has the Government considered purchasing and renting suitable housing to these people?

A: Now this you will regard as a bureaucratic answer and it probably is. The Agency is forbidden to operate within the continental limits of the United States. The matter of proper housing for African diplomats is, I believe, indeed I know, under urgent study by the State Department whose responsibility it is.

Q: Since your mandate relates to communication with peoples abroad, what does USIA do to train its representatives in foreign languages in order to communicate?

A: This is a constant problem in a country where the teaching of language is inadequate. We do now have training courses. In our recruitment we are putting increased emphasis on language training. We require to do much more of it. We require not only people who know foreign languages, but it is equally important that the people we send abroad have knowledge and information regarding their own country. If I had my way, I would insist that every American who goes abroad in an official capacity be required to purchase a secondhand automobile guaranteed to break down at least eight times in a small town as he drove from one coast to another, because I think the information he would acquire would be of great value to him abroad.

Q: Are you in urgent need of high talent volunteers from the US communications industry?

A: We are always in need of high class volunteers. The answer to the question is yes, particularly if they are familiar with the pay scale we are able to offer.

Q: Following that, do we understand that you need a larger appropriation? (Laughter)

A: When I first came down here I was advised by a man of great experience in Washington who said, in answering questions before committees or elsewhere, (1) never try to be funny; (2) never lie; and (3) never blurt out the complete truth. (Laughter from audience) This is, I am sure, not the forum to engage in a long-range discussion with the appropriation committees of the House and Senate. I would say this, however, that in our requests for funds for the coming fiscal year, we have asked for what we honestly believe we can spend effectively, efficiently, and without waste. But as we study the program, as we acquire real estate for new authorities, new facilities for book publishing, then in answer to the question, I would quote friends of mine in Brooklyn who were wont to say, "wait 'til next year," because we are going to ask for what we think the situation requires. And I would repeat again that the sum total of our requests now before Congress represents what we think we can spend effectively and efficiently.

Q: What can be done to obtain recognition abroad for over 56 billion dollars investment in economic aid?

A: I think we all know from traveling abroad that gratitude is almost as rare a commodity amongst nations as it is amongst individuals. We in the Agency have tried through print, film, television, to make clear the degree and extent of American economic aid. It, however, ought to be remarked that one cannot hammer too hard on recipient countries in a demand that they should express openly their gratitude for our generosity. No more can we reasonably expect nations to which we have acted as both midwife and fairy godmother to imitate us in all respects in their social and economic organization. The aid is given, as I understand it, in large measure to give them the economic, the educational opportunities to make a free choice without compulsions, just as the military aid is, in considerable extent, given in order that they may defend themselves. I do not mean to imply that we should downgrade our economic aid, but I do mean to say that to insist upon open expressions of great gratitude would, in this wonderful, wonderful word I've learned since coming to Washington…It would be counterproductive (Laughter), which as I understand it in old-fashioned logging terms would mean it would backfire. (Laughter and applause)

Q: Are there any plans for increased activities in South America other than Voice of America broadcasts?

A: There are indeed. Whatever happens to our amended budget, we shall put major emphasis on Latin America and on Africa. So far as Latin America is concerned, we now have a weekly newsreel on television that is carried in 15 countries, estimated audience 10 million. I am prepared to admit that estimate may be bloated, but I am familiar with bloated estimates from my domestic experience. (Laughter) We place some 1600 hours of radio per week on radio stations in Latin America and this, in the vernacular, is where we put the hay in the barn, because when you can get a program on a local medium-wave transmitter, then you are reaching the local audience. We shall increase our book translation program. We are going to start working, insofar as we can, with labor organizations. We hope to be able to do a certain amount of reporting of Latin America to itself, so that the increased emphasis of Latin America will by no means be confined to the Voice of America.

Q: Now continuing the broadcast view, moving to another continent however, do you think the "Courier" is a significantly useful instrument in the Voice of America program? Why?

A: The "Courier" was not a hundred percent successful. It was expensive to operate. Its signal was limited, and if pending negotiations are successful, we are going to move the transmitters ashore and either mothball or in some way, dispose of the "Courier." The change will increase our signal and reduce our costs.

Q: Has a film of our Astronaut been sent abroad? If so, why the original indecision reported in a newspaper column?

A: This is very embarrassing because the newspaper column was right, right in the sense that someone in our Agency said there was indecision. There was no indecision. We moved quantities of background material, both print and film, weeks ahead of the shot. Within roughly 26 hours of the shot we had a 10-minute film on the jets to every post abroad. We subsequently moved another 8-minute film, which gave the highlights of Commander Shepard's visit to Washington, his news conference and his acceptance of the medal from the president. So, as I say, this is a case where we did our job. The individual who wrote the piece did his job, but someone who was uninformed in the Agency conveyed the wrong impression. We are rather proud of what we did with that.

Q: It has been charged that USIA serves as a cover for CIA. Any comment? (Laughter from audience)

A: No. (More laughter from audience).... Just no.

Q: If USIA prestige poll was good enough to be used in a presidential campaign, why is it being dropped now, outside of the fact that there is no campaign?

A: It is quite true that we have abandoned the so-called prestige or barometer poll. The reason we did so was that we have no interest in spending the taxpayer's money to run a rating popularity between Mr.

Khrushchev and Mr. Kennedy. We shall continue to do some polling but the polling techniques will be used in an effort to discover and to determine the areas of interest, of curiosity, of apprehension, of misunderstanding. In short, an effort to find out what's bugging people about this country and its policies. And we shall also continue to make polls having to do with the impact of what we do, whether it be in films, television, or print on the recipient country. We shall also weld into that information acquired from a variety of sources because, as you gentlemen all know from experience, if someone puts on his hat and coat and goes and talks to a half dozen cabinet ministers and to six or eight newspaper editors in a foreign country, he is likely to acquire information as to reaction, or potential reaction, to a given line of policy, much more clearly than if he relies on public opinion polls. We also did not want to create the impression that United States foreign policy is being determined by holding the finger on the pulse of a rather limited popularity poll in a foreign country.

Q: Returning to the Cuban situation for a minute, please assess the propaganda effects of the "tractors for prisoners" affair?

A: Mr. President, I anticipated that such a question might arise. As you know, the President issued shortly before noon a statement on this subject, which is rather definitive. But it seems to me that, as Senator Smathers said I believe yesterday, that Castro's offer to exchange prisoners for tractors was a monumental propaganda blunder. The worldwide reaction was almost universally hostile. The obvious parallel was drawn all around the world between Castro's offer and the one made by Hitler when he offered to trade Jews for trucks. And this, I think, is significant—that Castro's offer has now been a running story for five days, and his friends in Moscow and Peiping have remained silent. Their radios are not commenting. The Communist press throughout the world is, in the main, observing what can only be described as a sort of embarrassed silence. Castro is now obviously attempting to recover from his blunder by saying he wants the tractors as indemnification for damage done. What he did initially, of course, was to demonstrate again to the world in dramatic fashion that the Communist machine operates without regard for those human values and human beings that are the hallmark of civilized society. And it seems to me that had American citizens remained mute and refused to act, they would, one, have denied their heritage and caused much of the world to believe that we value our dollars and machines above the freedom of men who are willing to risk their lives in an effort to regain freedom for their fellow countrymen.

I apologize for reading this, Mr. President, but I anticipated the question and rather wanted to say what I meant to say and sometimes in ad-libbing, I know from bitter experience, I do not. (Laughter and loud applause)

Q: Would a USIA Person-to-Person program, beamed into the homes of leaders of foreign states, be practical?

A: I really don't know. The program survived about seven years here and then succumbed. Some of them were, in fact, done in the homes of foreigners. I should think if the language problem could be overcome, and it could, technically speaking, that such a program might have some degree of acceptance. I really have not given that particular program any thought in recent years, Mr. President. (Audience laughter)

Q: Here's a quickie! Is a drive-in movie a worthy gain to Italy at USIA expense?

A: I suppose I could answer that as someone did once with what was called "an affirmative maybe." But I do not know that the drive-in theater was financed by United States funds and I should think the answer would be determined, in large extent, as to whether occasionally films produced by USIA were shown in the drive-in theater. (Laughter)

Q: Mr. Moses was here Monday and reported on the New York World's Fair. What is USIA's attitude on the World's Fair, and what is USIA doing to support the Fair?

A: I can quote to you from memory a letter from Charlie Poletti, who traveled pretty well around the world in promoting the World's Fair, and it said in substance that he had received efficient, effective, and invaluable cooperation from the USIA at posts around the world. It gives us pleasure to receive that kind of communication. We ourselves, as you know, are engaged in small fairs and exhibits abroad. We have a plastics exhibit in the Soviet Union that opened in Tashkent yesterday and the initial response was good. The answer is that we have made a substantial contribution toward encouraging foreign countries to show at New York's World's Fair.

Q: I have about five questions here. I think they're rather ones that you can handle quickly and we'll beat the two o'clock deadline. If we run over I'm sure it will be all right. We have a pretty rapt audience today. And this touches on the Press Club trip to Europe. About three hundred members will be flying over there on September first, for a vacation, and the question is: Has the USIA or the State Department weighed the impact of dumping more than 300 National Press Club members in London, simultaneously, on a single day in September?

A: Well London, as I know from experience, is a hospitable and gracious city, and whatever hardships may be experienced by former colleagues on this journey, I should hate to see the day come when USIA, the State Department or anyone else could say, "Don't go. There are too many of you!" I think the more, the better. (Laughter and applause)

Q: Isn't there some evidence that the New Zealers are beginning to display battle fatigue?

A: Sir, I regard that as a personal question. I accept it as such. And I'm afraid the answer may well be true. But I have noticed no signs of battle fatigue amongst my younger colleagues and a degree of tolerance for their more ancient associates. I have not noticed any slowing down of the tempo, although I must confess there have been times when I feel that we should commit ourselves to the proposition of the inevitability of gradualness. (Laughter) But I am much impressed with the stamina, the fortitude, and the steadiness of my colleagues. And the answer is that I have not yet seen any signs of battle fatigue, unless I see them while shaving in the morning. (Laughter)

Q: In a serious question, how can you explain the fact that some officers selected for your so-called Foreign Service Career Reserve suffered a pay cut for accepting what was supposed to be a form of promotion?

A: I said at the outset that when ignorance was obvious, I would confess it. My understanding is that this resulted as a result of a piece of legislation which did not turn out precisely as it was expected to turn out. The details of that I'm frankly not familiar with, but I have been taught to say, Mr. President, I would be glad to supply it for the record. I just don't know.

Q: It has been reported that you've been able to play golf only twice on your new job. Was it at Burning Tree and what did you shoot?

A: It was at Burning Tree. Once it was in company with Bill Lawrence, so I'm obliged to tell the truth lest he lie about it to you later. I pulled a tendon in my hand about a year ago running a bulldozer. (Laughter) On one occasion, due to the bad hand, I failed to finish the round, and on the other occasion I had 104. (Laughter)

Q: The handwriting is different but it's in the same vein. Are you now or have you ever been the best left-handed putter in Christendom?

A: I have not traveled all over Christendom or played all the courses. (Laughter) However, there was a time in my youth when I putted very well. That reference I think appeared in print under Scotty Reston's byline. And this I'm sure arose as the result of certain experiences we had during the war when we played a few times on courses that had given hospitality to unexploded bombs, and they had little ropes around them. And I never played golf very well, but I could putt well. Reston was a much better golfer and, occasionally, I could hold him even just by putting, so I think that is the reason for that. I should like to think it's true. (Laughter)

Q: And now before the last question, I have one here that you might have been prepared for. I don't know if you have a prepared note on it, but you might have expected it. I did. And the question is what do you think of Joe McCarthy now? (Laughter)

A: I did not expect the question. And I was taught…I think this is right…I was taught in my youth to say whatever one felt like saying about anyone who was living and had a chance to answer back. And I think that was pretty sound teaching. (Applause)

Q: Well, Sir, I'd like to present you with this Certificate of Appreciation for your coming here today and with a copy of the Press Club's First Fifty Year Book. Thank you, Sir. And the last question, is the job worse than with CBS in recent years? (Laughter)

A: The job is better. It is a combination of fascination mixed with occasional frustration. It is a mind stretching operation. It sometimes tends to strip the gears in the mind. I am, as I said earlier, happy in the work and in a goodly company, particularly here today. (Applause)

3. Radio Television News Directors Association, September 30, 1961

We have two ears and one mouth so that we can listen twice as much as we speak.
   Epictetus

Any student of American mass communications history must be aware of two bookend speeches of the mid-20th century that call upon our higher selves: Edward R. Murrow's "wires and lights in a box" speech at the Radio-Television News Directors Association annual meeting in Chicago on October 15, 1958, and Newton Minow's "vast wasteland" speech before the National Association of Broadcasters annual meeting in Washington, D.C., on May 9, 1961. Bookends are supports placed at each end of a row of books to hold them upright, and the Murrow/Minow bookend speeches are meant to provide much needed support to an industry that does not always stand upright.

Unlike Ed Murrow in 1958, Newton Minow in 1961 was not speaking to an industry full of peers, but rather as an attorney overseer who was Kennedy's first appointment to a regulatory agency, the Federal Communications Commission. The speech, referred to as the "Gettysburg Address for broadcasters,"[112] is still heavily cited fifty plus years later for its call to arms to elevate the public interest among those commercial providers who produce most of the content we think about:

> When television is good, nothing — not the theater, not the magazines or newspapers — nothing is better. But when television is bad, nothing is worse. I invite each of you to sit down in front of your television set when your station goes on the air and stay there for a day without a book, without a magazine, without a newspaper, without a profit and loss sheet or a rating book to distract you. Keep your eyes glued to that set until the station signs off. I can assure you that what you will observe is a vast wasteland.

The public responded well to Minow's speech. There were programs on television like "The Untouchables" that raised concerns about the level of violence and its impact on young minds. But some broadcasters felt threatened by this emboldened FCC chairman and sought to dig up some dirt on Minow. There wasn't any to find.[113] He was a Kennedy appointee who believed, as his boss did, that the federal government had a role to play in improving cultural programming. It was to be a New Frontier era in regulation and oversight, but of course with Kennedy's early death, it did not turn out that way.

In 1958 Murrow felt as if he could chastise his own kind—fellow journalists who would share his sense of outrage that not enough good quality programming was being offered, but even he, like Minow, would not be roundly applauded for publicly criticizing the media industry, which remains notorious for a lack of introspection about its roles and responsibilities.

It is understandable why Murrow took on the role of elder statesman for quality television. Murrow's See It Now (1951-1958) is considered the best that American primetime television has ever offered. It aired during television's Golden Age when the new centerpiece appliance of the den or living room fascinated the American family. An episode on the McCarthy era Communist-witch hunts involved Air Force reserve lieutenant Milo Radulovich, who had been discharged from the U.S. military for being associated with Communist sympathizer family members. After he and his father were interviewed for an October 1953 appearance on See It Now, Radulovich had his commission reinstated. On March 9, 1954, Murrow would initiate an investigation into Joseph McCarthy's tactics by airing excerpts from the senator's Congressional inquiries that showed the danger of overreach in a democratic republic and how such overreach played into the hands of enemies and target populations of American interest:

> This is no time for men who oppose Senator McCarthy's methods to keep silent, or for those who approve. We can deny our heritage and our history, but

> we cannot escape responsibility for the result. There is
> no way for a citizen of a republic to abdicate his
> responsibilities. As a nation we have come into our full
> inheritance at a tender age. We proclaim ourselves, as
> indeed we are, the defenders of freedom, wherever it
> continues to exist in the world, but we cannot defend
> freedom abroad by deserting it at home.
>
> The actions of the junior Senator from Wisconsin have
> caused alarm and dismay amongst our allies abroad,
> and given considerable comfort to our enemies. And
> whose fault is that? Not really his. He didn't create this
> situation of fear; he merely exploited it—and rather
> successfully. Cassius was right. "The fault, dear
> Brutus, is not in our stars, but in ourselves."[114]

When the last original broadcast of See It Now ran on July 7, 1958, it was also the last time a television host had almost complete autonomy with the content of his program. Television was under threat from the rise of the blockbuster movie-going audience. The drive to find the largest mass audience, a process that mandated a move to a lower common denominator, would take precedence over the drive for that higher self.

Thus Murrow was still licking his wounds and carrying the mantle for television's true potential, like a parent worried about how his kid was growing up, when he stepped before the RTNDA:

> This instrument can teach, it can illuminate; yes, and it
> can even inspire. But it can do so only to the extent that
> humans are determined to use it to those ends.
> Otherwise it is merely wires and lights in a box. There
> is a great and perhaps decisive battle to be fought
> against ignorance, intolerance and indifference. This
> weapon of television could be useful.[115]

In the following speech before the RTNDA, the new director of the United States Information Agency Murrow references Minow's wasteland speech in his opening remarks. The speech he gave before the same association in 1958 was not a "pilot" for his new Kennedy administration colleague. This Murrow, head of a government propaganda agency, is asking his former peers to consider their only real asset—credibility and integrity—and its value to telling America's story. He doesn't wish to tell them how to do their jobs, but just remind them of their awesome responsibility as information warriors on the frontline in news bureaus throughout the world.

Edward R. Murrow
Radio Television News Director Association
Washington, D.C.
September 30, 1961

It is three years since I have enjoyed the hospitality of this organization and we meet here in a city that breeds rumors. I would like to deny one at least, and that is that the remarks I made three years ago to this organization had represented a pilot for my colleague, Newt Minow. (Laughter)

You will forgive me if I read part of this dreary discourse, but I have discovered in the course of seven months that it is sometimes useful to know what one has said when in the presence of journalistic enterprise.

It is with a feeling of unaccustomed grace that I address you. This is due to the fact that within the memory of living men I was once one of you. We have all been colleagues of the Fourth Estate, all of us occupied in gainful pursuit at the bar of public opinion.

I am no longer one of those periodically writing and voicing those public memoranda of state to the president of the republic. And though I no longer number myself among the private voices of conscience, I trust you will regard me at least as a friend, and I hope, as a colleague still.

I am, as some of you may know, an alternative choice to the Secretary of State Dean Rusk. I should perhaps add the traditional phrase at this point that the opinions expressed here are not necessarily those of the

Secretary of State. But he did ask that his regards be conveyed. He was good enough to say that he was confident that you had made a happy choice.

But choices are not always happy ones. There is a tale told about the late Sir Thomas Beecham presiding at a rehearsal to which his principal oboist arrived very late, obviously in very bad shape after a heavy night. "Good morning," said Sir Thomas, to the pale and bleary oboist. "Now that you have safely found us, perhaps you would be good enough to give the orchestra your A note so that we can get on with our rehearsal." The unsteady oboist gingerly put his oboe into a dry, sour mouth. He blew into it. A half recognizable tone, which wobbled and oscillated, came out. And when it had at last perished into grateful silence, Sir Thomas turned accommodatingly to the orchestra and said, "Gentlemen, you may take your choice." (Laughter)

You, gentlemen and ladies, have taken your choice. It is I, and I trust that the note left in the mouth will not be too sour.

There is much that I could speak of tonight. Berlin is obviously uppercase in our headlines and uppermost in our apprehensions. Khrushchev's vicious vivisection of a city imperils the freedom of free men everywhere, both near and far. Here certainly ends the illusion that the defeated Germans lost the war and won the peace, for what prevails is certainly not peace.

But it is not Berlin alone about which I would speak to you, because your invitation to me said I could talk about anything that interested or excited me. One subject meets that qualification: the job I am trying to do.

So let us both have our choices. Let us combine your interest as news directors in Berlin with my interest as the director of the United States Information Agency.

I shall tell you what our Agency is, how it works and where possible use Berlin as the example.

Since you people work in sight and sound media, I want to give you the sight and sound of USIA by letting you see what it is that we daily send around the globe in the name of the people of this country. It is difficult for many of you to know just what our Agency does because our product is invisible; its goals are intangible.

What we do is solely for export. By Congressional mandate, we operate from the shores of this country outward. We are engaged in that vague, ill-defined area of telling America's story abroad, and of trying to turn politics into understanding.

In Brussels and in Bangkok, USIA officers explain the latest U.S. policy moves to newspaper editors. In the jungles of Southeast Asia, officers bring films and pamphlets to embattled Vietnamese counterinsurgents. In Laos, we have an officer who has a price on his head.

In steaming equatorial Africa other men teach English classes and share American know-how with people of newly sovereign nations.

On a towering South American plateau, USIA personnel run a lively binational community center and a library in a low-income neighborhood of Bogota.

What we endeavor is to reflect with fidelity to our allies, to the uncommitted nations, and even indeed to those who are hostile to us, not only our policy but also our ideals.

We not only seek to show people who we are and how we live. We must also engage others in the delicate, difficult art of human persuasion to explain why we do what we do.

To accomplish this we use many media of communication: radio, television, movies, newspapers, magazines, books, pamphlets, exhibits, trade fairs, the arts, teaching and education, personal contact, and above all, face-to-face conversation.

The range of expertise that we need in a Foreign Service officer is enough to make an educated man long for illiteracy.

But note that communications is only half our job. We deal as well in policy. We must make the policy of this government everywhere intelligible, and wherever possible, palatable.

We must speak in many languages to many peoples of vastly differing cultures and styles, of vastly differing levels of comprehension. For we speak not to a receiving, set saturated audience of one culture, in one country, speaking one language, as you ladies and gentlemen do.

Our media must talk both to peons and professors, to the illiterates of Central America, to the natives of Ghana, to the Muslim shopkeeper, to the Indian Hindu and to the Japanese scholar.

This means we must approach them in their own country, whatever its climate or terrain, in their own language, whatever its dialect, and on their own level, whatever its depth.

We must deal with the realities of their fears, their concerns, and their stereotypes of the product we promote, the hopes and actions of the United States Government.

This means that our work is endless and varied. Much of what we do is unglamorous and much of it thankless. In many areas apathy and suspicion are the enemies of understanding. Preconceptions about this country abroad abound. Much of what people think is distorted and unfavorable. Often our success is measured in good will gained or simply in the removal of ill will. Much of our work is long-term, quiet, and unsensational.

Since you are broadcasters, I would take this opportunity to tell you what we, the USIA, do in radio, films and television. I have told you a little about our radio operation. The question is, does anyone listen? Does anyone hear this shortwave stuff?

You will recall in 1959 when Khrushchev was in this country, two parents in Chicago stopped the Russian leader in a hotel and begged him to get their two children out of Soviet-held Lithuania. They had not seen the 20-year-old girl and the 16-year-old boy in fifteen years. Khrushchev agreed to do it. The Voice of America carried the story.

On a farm in Lithuania, the boy Toma was listening to the Voice and almost fell off his chair when he heard the announcer relay Khrushchev's promise about him and his sister, Regina. He quickly got confirmation that he was hearing correctly, for his neighbors from down the road came running to tell him the news, for they too had been listening.

Regina was working in a city over a hundred miles away. One of the neighbors was so excited he left immediately to give her the word, but the trip was unnecessary, for Regina had heard the story from friends of her own, all of whom had heard it from the Voice of America.

In 1960, large crowds in Bucharest, Rumania gathered in the city square enchanted in unison when the then orbited Echo 1 passed overhead. They shouted, "American satellite." How did they know of it? They heard the announcement of its time of passing overhead from the Voice of America.

I could tell you stories of this kind for hours, but we do know that we get through, because the Soviets take such pains to jam us. They have 2,000 jamming transmitters against our 87 sending transmitters. They spend well over 100 million dollars a year on jamming alone, more than six times our broadcasting budget and practically as much as the entire budget of the whole Agency.

We've been broadcasting for almost 20 years. We began within three months of the attack on Pearl Harbor when these first words were spoken in February of 1942. It was said then: "The Voice of America speaks. Today America has been at war for 79 days. Daily at this time we shall speak to you about America and the war. The news may be good or bad. We shall tell you the truth."

I consider it a point of personal pride that today we still aim our shots according to that mark. But it is a fact that on the broadcast firing line we are still outgunned by the opposition.

In total broadcast time, we rank fourth behind Radio Moscow, Radio Peking, and Radio Cairo. Some steps are being taken to correct this imbalance, which has grown over the last eight years. More will be suggested. All will take money.

We do not argue that more broadcasting alone will win the struggle, but in this unremitting war we wage for the wits of men, we must get our priorities straight and understand that to do what must be done may require an act of national self-discipline unprecedented in the history of this land.

I am, I suppose, shilling for the Agency I have the honor to head, but what you will next see is USIA Television, our newest medium, turning out more than 500 film reports and features annually. We air express tapes to 57 countries, serving 42 million foreign television sets, reaching an estimated audience of 150 million people. We do this with a staff of 64 people. Their hours are long, their budgets are low, but they are proud of their product, and we would show you a bit of it…if the system works.

[It did not work]

The only thing I can say about the technical quality of that production is something that you all have heard before, namely that when we looked at it and listened to it this afternoon it was leaving here alright. (Laughter) One more performance like that and I shall retire to the anonymity that so many people think I so richly deserve! From here on I shall be brief.

I have spent some of your time trying to tell you about my job and the product we turn out. We did not give a fair presentation of the product but that was due to conditions beyond our control. I think that's the old phrase, isn't it?

Give me just two minutes to share with you some of my thoughts about your work. As I said at the outset I tried to resist the temptation to tell you how to do your job. But I would suggest that if you are to discharge your responsibilities to your listeners, to your country, and your conscience, you must have more information about government policy and purpose, and not less.

For the responsibility that now rests upon you is greater than that which has burdened communicators at any time in the long history of communications. The speed of the instrument you use represents a hazard and puts a premium upon restraint, coolness, and mature judgment. For your audience, in varying degrees, believes in you and trusts you. They probably think you know more than you do. But your credibility, your integrity represents your only real asset.

This country is now in a position where decisions must be made in an arena that is illuminated by the bright lights of television, where there is little time for hesitation. We have no cushion, as we have had in the past, in terms of time or distance. For there will be no opportunity for those who are half asleep to become half ready. This is part of the price of leadership and part of the burden we bare as a result of the speed and power of modern weapons.

Let me illustrate the change that has occurred by revealing what is perhaps a small footnote to the history of recent communications. Shortly after the outbreak of war in 1939, the majority of United States radio networks and certain government officials decided to terminate all news broadcasts from Europe. They were fearful, lest emotional strain or physical danger would cause reporters to violate neutrality, agitate for action, or otherwise compromise the isolation, the detachment, which we were determined to defend.

That decision did not stand for more than 48 hours, but it was taken.

Now as we face squarely the prospect of another and more terrible war, that question at least will not arise. But the old question that has troubled thoughtful men since speech began, remains: What to say and how to say it. And the how can be as important as the what.

We are approaching a time when the steadiness, the fortitude of this country will be tested as never before. Our nerves are going to be twisted and tortured. And we shall at some point be required to reach a collective conclusion as to whether we are prepared to pay another installment in the unending and escalating price of freedom.

It is going to require an act of national self-discipline that is without precedent. And this appraisal, this estimate of the worth of what we have must be carried out with the freedom of expression and reporting that is known in no other country. That is our way of doing things, and the way it is done is largely your responsibility.

You represent relatively new instruments of communication, but I have occasionally felt that you all too frequently have made your youth your oldest excuse for your shortcomings. You have the power and therefore you have the responsibility.

Maturity is not measured by age but by performance.

I would not like to be misunderstood. This is no plea for conformity or uncritical acceptance and support of the policies of this administration. I hope that seven months or seven years as a bureaucrat will not change lifelong convictions.

But I do suggest there isn't going to be any need in the coming months for anyone to hot up his copy or to exaggerate the importance of events. There are and there will be disagreements between this government and its allies. I am not suggesting they should not be reported, but rather put in perspective, with full recognition that the primary and consistent pattern of Russian policy for more than a decade has been to sunder the Western Alliance.

Honorable and dedicated men in this country will differ regarding the policies we should pursue. I am not suggesting that these differences should be ignored or glossed over. I am saying that our enemies and our allies will be watching us, the way we talk, the manner in which we conduct ourselves, as never before.

In the coming months, you and the people who work for you will be writing and speaking not only a footnote to history but what could be the final chapter. I have worked intimately with many of you. I know the manner of man you are, and have some knowledge of the power and the influence you possess.

So far as news is concerned, most of you will, I am sure, continue to try to get it first but first get it right. But I think the times require a recognition of a new responsibility. The responsibility rests uniquely upon you, simply because you are so few, and because you are in fact the eyes and ears of your fellow countrymen.

I am not suggesting that you all become somber sentinels intoning events and pronouncements of a magnitude beyond the grasp of most men. A little gaiety goes well with grimness, and in the past, sane men have been able to tinge adversity with humor.

Perhaps I could have said what I'm trying to say with greater brevity by merely telling you a story, but I'm rather reluctant to confess that I have reached the age where my own reminiscences fascinate me. However, it was all summed up early one morning after one of the roughest nights of the London Blitz. I had been driving about all night in an open car with an elderly reporter, a man of great wisdom and a degree of cynicism. And when we came back at first light, sat down at our typewriters, I confessed the obvious by saying to him, "I don't know how to write the story." He said, "It's very simple, my boy, it's very simple. Just sit down and write it as though it were your last one, because you know, it just might be.

4. Forum Dinner with Hollywood, November 5, 1961

Hollywood never knew there was a Vietnam War until they made the movie.
        Jerry Stiller

9039 Beverly Boulevard in West Hollywood is today a Bristol Farms known for its extraordinary gourmet food at extraordinary prices. You may even come across a celebrity squeezing a cantaloupe.

On November 5, 1961, the address was the site of the world-famous Chasen's restaurant for what could have been called *Mr. Murrow Goes to Hollywood.* The Hollywood speech was Murrow's idea and arranged by the Academy of Motion Picture Arts and Sciences, the same organization that presents one of the most watched global media events, the Academy Awards, better known as the Oscars.

Murrow began by saying *he felt* he was among friends. Perhaps that was his first mistake.

In attendance that night were Paul Newman, Marlon Brando, Frank Capra, John Wayne, John Ford, David Selznick, Samuel Goldwyn, among other luminaries. It was said to be the hottest ticket in town.[116]

Murrow sat at the head table with Eric Johnston, president of the Motion Picture Association of America (MPAA). Fourteen years earlier in November 1947, Johnston had convened a meeting of 48 motion picture executives at New York's Waldorf-Astoria Hotel, which led to The Waldorf Statement. In it, Hollywood executives deplored the actions of the Hollywood 10 who were cited in contempt by the House of Representatives for refusing to confirm or deny membership or affiliation with Communists. The Waldorf Statement promised to eliminate Communist subversives and disloyal Americans from its industry. Johnston had more recently appeared on Murrow's 1958 CBS program, *Small World*, which cast seemingly opposite types in conversation with Murrow from their respective global locations. It was a technological wonder at the time to use international phone lines and location cameramen who filmed each guest in person and then have the film flown to New York for editing down to a 30-minute program. Johnston appeared as head of the MPAA from Washington with the actress Lauren Bacall from Hollywood and Malcolm Muggeridge, former editor of *Punch*, retired and living in Australia.

Lauren Bacall recalls a pre-production meeting for Small World with Murrow in New York where he expressed his unease with her calling him a "big star." In anger he replied, "I'm not a star. I'm a journalist."[117] And now as head of the U.S. Information Agency, Murrow was neither a Hollywood star nor a journalist but a government bureaucrat.

Edward R. Murrow took his last bite of a Chasen's meal and stood before the other "stepchildren of modern communications" who worked in the celluloid industry. It was Sunday, November 5, 1961, and just like his famous 1958 speech before the Radio Television News Directors Association three years earlier, Murrow brought along his moralist compass. The trouble was, no one was asking for directions to his morality play.

One almost expected to hear, "This just might do nobody any good." Chasen's restaurant was a cozy glitterati locale known for its good chili. Plenty of adult beverages flowed amidst deals and gossip. Much noshing and glad handling between the honorific former celebrity journalist, however uncomfortable the label, and Hollywood filmmakers likely preceded this speech. In Hollywoodland, everyone loves a party, and Mr. Murrow was as much a film star on the small screen as any other from the big screen.

Long a favorite meeting place for Old Hollywood A-listers like Bob Hope, Frank Sinatra, Jimmy Stewart, and Liz Taylor, Chasen's would that night become the site of a showdown between the journalist-turned-America's image czar and the storytellers whose global influence—for good and bad—extended well beyond entertainment value. Their work in Hollywood, Murrow would preach, was about America's national security.

Murrow was no longer just one who had engaged in reporting and editing for most of his life. He was no longer just the observer and commentator. He was not even the host of his celebrity-friendly *Person to Person*, where he took long drags on his omnipresent cigarette between friendly but bored banter with stars showcasing their homes.

Fundamentally, he wasn't really "one of them," as he was not known to make the social circuit among the rich and famous. He was now wearing a brand new hat: the foreign policy decision maker, undoubtedly very serious that night, but cautious to go too far lest he lose his friendly audience. In West Coast eyes, go too far he did, and he left as many a Washington federal official leaves Hollywood—with heavier shoulders.

As with any good persuasive speechmaker, Murrow began with a promise not to overstep his boundaries. He would not poke his nose into other people's business. He wasn't there to enforce anything related to how Hollywood ran its ship of takes. He was the poster child of the First Amendment. And after all, didn't Hollywood operate free of any government oversight, save foreign export quotas? But then he broke his promise, or at least bent it sharply: "It is important that you understand this. My purpose is not to pillory an industry at fault with its function." He then went on to make one judgment and then another.

The smatterer cast smatterings that left Hollywood squirming in its seats. His healthy criticism of unhealthy Hollywood wasn't going down well.

He implied the "R" word and crossed it with a "T": Responsibility in an age of Terror. Hollywood was free to make its pictures however it wanted, but it had to acknowledge that it had a shared responsibility for how those pictures would influence and shape U.S. foreign policy and public opinion abroad.

One can imagine how high the temperature increased in the room.

Who was *this* Edward R. Murrow, champion of liberal idealism, who used his electronic bully pulpit in the 1950s to take on the conservative reactionary Joseph McCarthy? He had declared in 1954: "This is not time for men who oppose Senator McCarthy's methods to keep silent...we cannot defend freedom abroad by deserting it at home."[118] Then a stunned silence in Hollywood these seven years later.

Perhaps this Murrow of the 1960s must have sounded McCarthyesque in his dour conclusions: "We live in an age of terror. No man can see the end of it." Hollywood's responsibility to America and its face to the world was nothing short of profound, to borrow Murrow's word. People who may not be able to read and write can still see a film and feel like they "know" the people behind those images. The celluloid is their real world. "But doesn't this disturb you?" asks Murrow. People abroad know the United States largely through the prism of Hollywood. "Are you satisfied with the way you have pictured America as a place to live?"

That night, Mr. Murrow in Hollywood called for restraint. Look before you leap. Think about the stories you tell and the characters you portray, especially those of the continents increasingly important to the Kennedy administration's foreign policy: Africa and Latin America.

The news reports from that night were not full of the same opprobrious tone as the messenger at Chasen's. UPI's headline was misleading, if not defensive: "Film Exports Decried: Murrow Says U.S. Movies Give False View of Nation." The wide distribution of American movies overseas has persuaded many foreigners that Chicago is still wracked by gang wars, that Indians still ride to war in the West and that a woman without a 40-inch bust cannot be an American.[119]

In "Hollywood Error," Murray Schumach wrote, "Edward R. Murrow came to Hollywood...preceded by an aura of suspicion and left a cloud of bewilderment."[120] Not a good forecast for building bridges of understanding between Hollywood and Washington.

Film critic Bosley Crowther questioned what is healthy fare in

Hollywood: "...it would be helpful if Mr. Murrow would define what he and his associates in the Government consider a "healthy image" to be. Do they consider the image—or images—presented by such films as "The Apartment," "Anatomy of a Murder," "Cat on a Hot Tin Roof," "The Defiant Ones," "West Side Story," "Splendor in the Grass," "Bad Day at Black Rock," and "A Raisin in the Sun" to be good, constructive propaganda for this country abroad?[121] All of these films, he argued, were deemed among Hollywood's best fare in quality storytelling, but the reflection on the United States was not always rosy—it was violent, bigoted, small-minded, and even drunk. Even "Mr. Smith Goes to Washington" was about the political machine that can ruin a man's idealism. "The best thing about American movies is their freedom to expose and criticize that which is not good about us," concluded Crowther.

Journalists spotlighted what was wrong with Murrow's critique, but missed the landscape view. Perhaps the press missed the whole point of Murrow's speech because they were barred from attending the event; they had to work off the reaction of those who attended and a press release of Murrow's remarks.

Murrow was asking an industry with which he felt much kinship to look within, examine the consequences of its own product, an examination as much about how foreigners are cast as how they are persuaded. In short, he was telling America that its story must not be so self-serving. Global problems threatened and all Americans should do their part to contribute to the American cause.

This was the year of the Bay of Pigs Fiasco, the Berlin Wall Crisis, and the first posting of American "military advisers" in a country that would soon be known to all Americans as Vietnam. New, but fragile, democracies were emerging in Africa and elsewhere. While Cuba embarrassed the United States, the Soviets won the propaganda war that spring with the first manned spaceflight before John Glenn's historic flight around the world could restore the balance in space power.

Murrow's "free advice" seems to have come at great cost. Hollywood that night was not open to his judgment that America's image vis-à-vis Hollywood "was not always a healthy one and self-restraint may nowadays be a good prescription."

Said Mr. Schumach: "A harsh critic will provoke an initial response of fury. But if he is right, the ultimate reaction will be one of respect from those men in Hollywood who are intelligent, creative and, in the long run, the pattern-setters of the industry. Subtlety makes more sense in diplomacy than in Hollywood."

The final judgment was in: Murrow had been too harsh on Hollywood.

There was at least one there that night who thought Murrow was right and told him so. Marvin Wald was a freelance documentary filmmaker and later a screenwriter who received an Academy Award nomination for the film, "The Naked City." Wald watched as none other than Eric Johnston rose from his head table with Murrow and proceeded to denounce Murrow's conclusions. Johnston said that the vast majority of the world's peoples drew favorable conclusions from American films. They liked that the United States wasn't afraid to show its true colors, warts and all. The world had high respect for America's ideals of free speech and free press. Wald witnessed a Hollywood producer follow Johnston's comments with a suggestion that Murrow's turn as bureaucrat had turned him into a Hollywood censor the way his once nemesis Joe McCarthy had done to the entire country. Wald writes, "Murrow was accused of deserting his journalistic ideals to become a government apologist. He was reminded that Hollywood would follow only the rule of the marketplace. Whatever made money would be produced. Hollywood was not a propaganda mill town."[122]

Murrow's departure from Chasen's was ignoble. No one spoke to him as he headed for the exit. Wald managed to corral Murrow and describe an inspiring new documentary film, "The Rafer Johnson Story," about the African American Gold Medal decathlete who served as UCLA student body president. Journalist Mike Wallace, before his *60 Minutes* career, narrated it. Wald said that this type of film could tell a positive story about America to the world.

Two weeks after that tough night, USIA Director Murrow wrote Wald: "You will be glad to know that we have already purchased several prints of The Rafer Johnson Story for use in our Motion Picture Program in Nigeria and Ghana in advance of Rafer Johnson's visits to these countries. Also we are presently negotiating for translation rights to permit wider distribution through our film libraries overseas. We consider The Rafer Johnson Story a very valuable film in our program. May I add that I appreciate your understanding and cordial comments concerning my recent remarks in Hollywood."

Edward R. Murrow
Forum dinner with representatives of the film industry in Hollywood
Chasen's Restaurant
November 5, 1961

It is not often that I come to dine and speak among friends. There are faces here that I know well. We all of us share in common the fact that we are the stepchildren of modern communications. We have supped together, and it is with the pleasant taste of cuisine still on my palate that I recall Ambrose Bierce's definition of the word, "Abdomen: the Temple of the God Stomach, and whose worship, with sacrificial rights, all true men engage."

And we men, true and now well fed, are also known as connoisseurs of the fine art of taste and entertainment. I can never forget that tale of the ultimate in the art of "connoisseur-manship." An old wine bibber had been smashed in a railway collision. Some wine was poured upon his lips to revive him. He opened his eyes, murmured "Château Margaux, 1937" and then died.

I can already imagine in that sometime year of nineteen-never-sixty a connoisseur of films, in sheer ecstasy at the delight before his eyes on the screen, keeling over with the words on his lips, "Sam Goldwyn, 1957," and then passing out never to be revived.

It was also Ambrose Bierce who described a connoisseur as a specialist who knows everything about something and nothing about anything else.

I appear here as a "smatterer." One who has spent most of his life as a reporter and editor and who is now privileged to participate in certain decisions regarding U.S. foreign policy and then to attempt the explanation and exposition of those policies abroad.

It will come, I am sure, as no surprise to you gentlemen to learn that you and your product are well known abroad. Half or more of the adult population of, for example, Britain, France, and Italy and a third in West Germany have seen American movies. Outside this country 150,000,000 tickets are bought each week to see Hollywood films. The bulk of screen time throughout the world is devoted to showing American films, for better or for worse, and in some areas it runs as high as 90 percent.

I am not here to tell you how to run your business, what pictures to make or how to make them. It is dangerous to give advice—fatal to give good advice—and so I suggest that we might usefully talk together as to how we may together enlist our talents and our toil in the service of our country.

You control or greatly influence an instrument of communication of great power and versatility. You operate and you export without control or coercion except insofar as foreign governments impose quotas. You compete for the attention of the world with all others who make pictures that move. You ask no subsidy from the government and the government seeks to exercise no control over you.

That is as it should be. However, all men who communicate, regardless of the instruments they use, now share a common problem. That problem is the survival of free men. I bandy no words when I say these are testing times, and in the times ahead there may be even greater tests of our will to survive. What I am suggesting is that this problem concerns you in Hollywood as much as it does us in Washington.

It is important that you understand this. My purpose is not to pillory an industry at fault with its function. Quite the contrary, much of the image of America around the world is due to the American film. You have in your product communicated our sense of generosity, our large-heartedness, our capacity for change, our egalitarian ideal that here a man is a man, our horizon of opportunity, our sense of growth and concern.

I myself have not yet reached the age where my own reminiscences fascinate me. But I have seen certain crises and conflicts and have at times been moderately well paid for observing how men and women conduct themselves under such conditions. There was Vienna at the time of the Anschluss—the betrayal of Czechoslovakia—Dunkirk—the British Expedition to Norway—the Blitz in London—and that year when Britain fought alone. There was North Africa, Normandy, Buchenwald and Dachau, the first months of the war in Korea, too many international conferences to count. The brief periods of tranquility are lost in the memory of turmoil.

And yet I am persuaded that new crises of greater magnitude impend. Decisions of great complexity and greater consequence are just over the horizon. Our oceans have become rivers, our dreams have become doubts, and the very atmosphere is harsh.

We live in an age of terror. No man can see the end of it. This state of perpetual crisis will inevitably produce a certain sense of frustration in a people accustomed to seek and find with few exceptions easy and quick solutions to our national problems. The times require an act of national self-discipline that is wholly unprecedented in our history. We must avoid the peaks of optimism and the valleys of despair and must recognize that we have no cushion in terms of time or distance.

It is long since this country has suffered or sacrificed. It is long since our ability to stand steady in our shoes in time of adversity has been tested. I suggest that the testing time approaches. If we are to meet that test—and all previous crises must be regarded as prelude to it—then we must combine patience with fortitude. We must recognize that there are no easy answers and that difficulty is an excuse history never accepts.

The immediate flashpoint is Berlin. It is a crisis of worldwide dimensions and the result will determine whether the hypothesis upon which this country was created will survive.

As we are nibbled at in Berlin, in Laos, Vietnam and elsewhere, there will be those who look about for domestic scapegoats, those who say let us imitate the Communists. Let us resort to threat and terror, rely only on force, forget about world opinion, silence dissent and argument in this country. In the very process of protecting liberty we could lose that which we are preparing to defend.

It was, I believe, Adolf Hitler who said that the great strength of the totalitarian state was that it would force those who feared it to imitate it.

There are those who demand a restatement of our national purpose. I suggest it is not needed. The basic papers are still there—the Bill of Rights might evoke debate, but in the end it would still pass the present Congress.

The present danger is that men who have known freedom, who have been nourished on it, and those who are experiencing it for the first time may be tempted to make peace with their fears. They may be terrorized into terminating their responsibility for making the tough individual decisions. They may conclude that material things are in the saddle, that the individual is helpless and his influence unfelt.

In this climate, what my Agency USIA does or what Hollywood does will not determine the course of world history. But a contribution can be made. I am fully aware of the contribution made by Hollywood in the late great war and in Korea. You were generous and unstinting of your time and your talent. The Republic is in greater danger now than even during those wars.

For then mistakes could be retrieved. Only battles hung in the balance.

But now the balance weighs civilization itself. The foe we face is skillful and implacable. He is able to operate on the world scene with every device of deceit, terror, and bribery. He is able to operate ventures for political purposes at an economic loss. He is able to deny his own people knowledge of his own acts or the reaction to them. And we must compete in cold blood and in freedom.

I can add that the political competition thinks rather highly of what you do. It was Joseph Stalin who said: "The cinema is the greatest means of mass agitation. The task is to take it into our hands." It was a man by the name of Lenin who said earlier: "Of all the arts, for us the most important one is the cinema." And Joseph Stalin also is reported once to have remarked about the people who sit in this room: "If I could control the medium of the American motion pictures I would need nothing else in order to convert the entire world to Communism."

If you come so well regarded by the opposition you are an asset too valuable to lose.

It was a little more than a week ago tonight that Carl Sandburg came to Washington at the request of the President's Cabinet and Mrs. Kennedy. He sat with us, he read to us, and he sang to us. With a heart still young in a breast not yet aged this 82-year-old son of the hills of America had something to say that I think worth mentioning to you gentlemen and ladies. I give you his exact words:

> I meet people occasionally who think that motion pictures, the product that Hollywood makes, is merely entertainment, has nothing to do with education. That's one of the darndest fool fallacies that is current. When I was a motion picture editor on the Chicago Daily News we used to report what was a four handkerchief picture as distinguished from the two handkerchief picture. Anything that brings you to tears by way of drama does something to the deepest roots of your personality. All movies good or bad are educational and Hollywood is the foremost educational institution

on earth, an audience that runs into an estimated 800 million to a billion. What, Hollywood, more important than Harvard? The answer is, not as clean as Harvard, but nevertheless, farther reaching.

Movies can and do have an extraordinary impact upon peoples in the emerging lands. Film potential for accomplishment is as limitless as the human imagination for which it serves as fuel.

Going even further, the impact of movies on illiterate societies can be profound. If a man cannot read or write, seeing and experiencing are his only paths to knowledge. Many an African owes his present level of general knowledge to foreign films. For example, in four West African cities among those who cannot read almost 40 percent are regular moviegoers. These people learn what they never knew before, and they also learn to advance what they already know.

But doesn't this disturb you? Pause a moment, and consider the proposition that whatever these people know of the United States they have largely learned from Hollywood's product. Are you satisfied with the way you have pictured America as a place to live? I shall resist the temptation of adopting the critic's garb and reciting an indictment of alleged movieland ills. But I shall make one comment. There are many people abroad who think that Chicago is still wracked by gang warfare, that the West is still wild, that beyond the Mississippi lie badlands still periled by warring Indians, that all other Americans live in penthouse apartments, drive limousine-dimension convertibles, wear tailored furs, and that any woman without a 40 inch bust and 20 inch waist and any man not gilded with the golden head of Adonis must not be an American. How do they know all this? They say they saw it in the movies.

Going even further, many Africans regard Hollywood films as portraying an African Adam and Eve living in an American conceived Garden of Evil. Many Hollywood films paint Africa as being only untracked jungle, ferocious tribesmen, savagery and ignorance dominating an existence of squalor by people rooted in their own primitiveness.

One American film company, for an African epic, flew animals from New York City to Africa for its picture. The message implied: wild animals are at home among Africans, and they should be pictured together. African tribesmen in gaudy dress and warpaint carry spears and shields and dance in a background of shouts and warwhoops. The message: Africans are an unintelligent menial lot obsessed with a bloodthirsty lust. In another film an African is savagely clubbed to death by a member of a rival tribe. The message: bestiality is the sole prerogative of Africans. Still another film showed an American hunter who left his young son in the care of a "trusted" African servant but when he returned he found his son slain by a gang led by the same African. The message: when Africans work under white men, they are good and peaceful; when the white men leave, violence erupts and they kill.

This last film incidentally concluded its story line with this American revolting from any control by local British administration, tracking the assailant through the jungle, killing in the course of his search a lion, a buffalo, crocodiles, and assorted animals, and finding time between killings for a passion-provoked love affair. Quite a lesson, you must agree, for this country to be exporting to Africa.

This may appear to you to be a caricature. But I have caricatured your pictures, and what they do, no more than some of your pictures have caricatured the way of life they purport to present.

I try to view this not only through my eyes but through the eyes of Africans I have met. I need hardly add that when Africans view such films about their lands and their lives they hardly stand up and cheer with delight.

But this goes further. Africans remember their "colonial" past, but African eyes are trained on the present and how it molds the future. In an era when they struggle to gain independence to join the family of nations, they regard such films as propaganda used by accomplices of the "colonizers" to support the argument that Africans are too immature to rule themselves. Africans do not appreciate the implicit message of many films that no African society is capable of independent intelligent leadership without white advice.

One final thought about Africa and Hollywood movies. Africa today is neither Communist nor capitalist. Africa is ambitious. Its people would, either with or without our help, seek relief from a crushing way of existence. They observe in the produce of Hollywood the progress that has been the hallmark of this wide and capacious land: huge factories, endless highways, innumerable automobiles, massive skyscrapers, countless machines, a land, in fact, so abundant that units of measure sometimes give way to adjectives in the superlative degree: the biggest, largest, longest, widest, hugest, in one word, the most.

Africa, too, is a wide land, and if preliminary estimates are an indication, it is, like our country, capaciously endowed. Having seen our abundance, they would seek our assistance in their struggle to emancipate peoples from poverty. If we join them, Hollywood and this land must learn a lesson. We must not divide men into primitive and civilized, superior and inferior. Those labels only justify the cult of injustice, self-aggrandizement, the exercise of power. This minor planet on which we live is inhabited by men. There is no primitive or civilized man. Some men live in primitive conditions, others in civilized conditions. But there is only one species of man on the earth.

Much of your output is probably beyond the realm of our discussion tonight. You are engaged essentially in the business of entertainment, and this is no unsavory undertaking. To give relief for a few small coins from the tedium and toil that is life on so much of our globe is a worthy goal. As one of our USIA posts reported in a dispatch: "This country's theatergoers prefer light entertainment to thought-provoking themes."

But in seeking to entertain I wonder if on occasion you do not permit acceptability to outweigh desirability. I wonder how much truth there is if we compare the celluloid world of America with the real world of America. I can also quote another dispatch from a USIA post abroad: "The picture of a grasping, materialistic U.S. society is everywhere to be seen by the lower classes for about 10 to 20 cents a ticket."

The box office proves that your basic product appeals to people. Let me share with you this dispatch from Latin America: "Films dealing with crime, violence, horror and sex usually give unfavorable impressions of life in the United States. However, regardless of the impressions received, moviegoers seem to enjoy American films thoroughly."

But let me be blunt about this. Films may provide a high level of audience enjoyment and at the same time convey an equally high level of negative impressions about the United States. Because audiences like the extremities of storytelling is no reason to feed them that to the exclusion of all else. Children like candy. They will eat it to excess if fed only that. But no man in his right mind would prescribe a diet of chocolate bars and ice cream. Self-restraint and control make a healthy child. I suggest that the image conveyed abroad of our land is not always a healthy one, and self-restraint may nowadays be a good prescription.

If we were to postulate, and I submit that this is true, that we are engaged in a great competition for the minds of the struggling peoples of the globe, what we present to those minds may be more than important. It may be vital. In many corners of the globe the major source of impressions about this country are in the movies they meet. Would we want a future-day Gibbon or Macaulay recounting the saga of America with movies as his prime source of knowledge? Yet for much of the globe, Hollywood is just that—a prime, if not sole, source of knowledge. If a man totally ignorant of America were to judge our land and its civilization based on Hollywood alone, what conclusions do you think he might come to? Opinions may differ. I for one am not optimistic about the result.

Preposterous, you say. It is entertainment. People see it, accept it and judge it on the basis of light fiction alone. They must know that the West is not wild, that we do not live with horror, that terror, sex, sin, and violence is not the daily way of American life, that there is another side to our land than all this celluloid make-believe.

I suggest they do not know the contrary.

Come look over my shoulder again at some of the papers on my desk about the impact of Hollywood abroad.

From Thailand a study of several thousands of the well-educated Thailand citizens—the "elite" of that country. They had seen American pictures, and 40 percent of them believed that they were given a true picture of our country. Another 8 percent said they thought the picture of America was "partly true." Do you realize this means half the educated people of that pivotal Southeast Asian country believe that the film America is the real America?

From Indonesia: "The majority of the Indonesian population is still illiterate… The masses learn of America and of our American way of life from moving pictures. They are to a large extent pictures of crime and violence… pictures cruelly distorting our way of life… This is a deplorable argument against us that we ourselves furnished to our communist enemies; an argument vivid, strong, hardly forgettable."

Forty-six visitors from 18 countries—foreign leaders brought to this country—were asked about American movies. Note this interesting figure: Four out of five of them said that movies were the source of images about this country held by their countrymen and that the masses of people in their homeland believed what they saw.

To personalize it a bit more, sample these comments from individual foreign leaders speaking of U.S. movies in their lands:

From India: "Movies are doing a lot of harm to America. They convey the notion that America is a country of millionaires and crooks."

From Latin America: "Movies are a terrible influence… South Americans take the American movies seriously. They think everything they see is true."

From Southeast Asia: "Movies misrepresent… we think of American housewives as useless drones always smoking and drinking cocktails."

Those are extreme opinions, some naïve. But the important thing is not what we think about their thoughts, but the fact that they think as they do about our land.

My concern about their opinions arises from a deep conviction that what others believe about us is important, indeed may be decisive. It is currently fashionable to discount "world opinion." If we come to hold world opinion in contempt then we may conclude that the opinion of the individual in our own country is of no account. It is true that our arsenal of nuclear weapons is adequate to any demands that may be made upon it. If it comes to a killing match, those of us who are left in this generous and capacious land will have won it. Meanwhile, we must persuade lest we and millions elsewhere perish. Those who communicate are responsible for what is communicated.

You have already played a large role. I want you now to suggest an even greater role. In times like these everyone has more responsibilities than makes him comfortable. But as these are uncomfortable times so must we shoulder uncomfortable burdens.

Ours is the burden of world leadership. I will be candid and observe that the deep concern—even the passion—with which American movies are regarded is but a tribute both to you and to the United States. A movie by any other name from any other country would still be a movie, but not subject to near so rigorous an inspection. But people around the world feel that their fates will largely be determined by what we here do or do not do.

Having here introduced the verb form, "to do," let me mention some of my own ideas about what can be done in this relentless world of ours.

First, let me puncture an objectionable balloon before it is inflated. That's the subject of censorship.

I have talked with many foreigners and some Americans abroad and from their comments arises more than just a passing appetite to censor. They firmly insist that somebody should control the export of

Hollywood.

I have always countered this appetite to censor with a few simple questions. Who is to do the censoring? Once you begin, where do you stop? Why not apply it to books, to magazines, television and radio, as well as films? Why not in the end of the day apply it to human beings, the best communicators of all? Censorship is no answer. It has no terminal point. It would be a denial of the hypothesis upon which this country was created and it would destroy the very human institutions which we now defend. But it is in our tradition and I think entirely permissible in this type of discourse for a government official to suggest that those who export films should recognize that in the kind of implacable savage competition in which we are now engaged, celluloid represents a strategic commodity. Weapons of discredit and distortion should not be placed in the hands of our enemies or before the eyes of our friends.

I trust this will not be regarded as in any way a plea for a great outpouring of films of social significance designed to improve the image of the United States abroad. Merely to entertain is to create a favorable climate of opinion. But it is not a totally entertaining world in which we reside. You have the overwhelming power both to entertain and to inform.

I would be bold enough to suggest that the history of this land, done as only your skills could do it, could reap great benefits abroad and solidify the purpose of our own people. We are in a period of great crisis and in time of crisis modern nations go back to their rootholds and examine the very essence from which they came. It was not accident that during the Battle of Britain, the posters carried a quote from Elizabeth the First, that the BBC's theme came from Cromwell's great marching song, General de Gaulle reached for the Cross of Lorraine as his symbol with the sure instinct of a man who knew his history and his people. Even the Russians in the dark days, when German armor cut like a scythe through their country, forgot about orthodox Communist doctrine and went back to Peter the Great and Suvorov. In desperate days people are what they have been. They desire to be worthy of their ancestors who suffered, sacrificed and achieved the degree of dignity and independence they now enjoy.

A type of cavalcade of America would help immeasurably abroad. An intense curiosity around the world raises more questions about this country than we can ever answer. We answer them in words. You can answer them in pictures. What I have in mind is an epic on America, a travelogue to end all travelogue, the trip that any reasonably intelligent man would take, showing what we are like, how we live, and what we do.

Parenthetically, I might add that commercial films made by Pan American and Greyhound some years back are still important weapons in any film arsenal that translates America abroad.

Further, there is going on around the periphery of Communism a centrifugal type of action with people spilling out at all corners. Refugees flow from Cuba, from Tibet, from Berlin and Hungary. I have talked with some of these people. If there is drama among human beings, there is drama here. Must we wait for an event to become history to turn to it?

What more dramatic excitement could one wish than the vicious vivisection of a city by the Ulbricht wall in Berlin? Or ranging back a few years, the Hungarian revolution in 1956, the Poznan riots in Poland, the East Berlin uprising in '53, or for that matter, the Berlin airlift in 1948. If you want to be on the front lines of the War of Confrontation between our way of life and the Soviet, the subjects are as numerous as there are people to live them. And there are literally millions of people living them every week of the year.

Is there a reason not to have films on the Allied Alliance in the last war, showing the efficacy of alliances and the agreements the Russians solemnly swore to and just as solemnly broke?

American politics itself could bear explaining. Illustrate, for example the drama of a citizen protest bringing about a political result. This is democracy in the raw, and it is democracy in the United States.

The world is inordinately cautious about our scientific achievements. My agency provides all the information it can, and it is still not enough. Hollywood could dramatically turn its lights to American superiority in science, and all of us would share the gain.

I have yet to see a picture where anyone ever pays taxes. We are asking people abroad, most immediately in Latin America, to make sacrifices for the good of us all. They conceive of these requests as coming from America, the land of the plush, where everyone is so rich no sacrifices are needed. A little bright white light on this would help as well.

There have been cables from posts abroad commenting on the exquisitely inept fare offered by this country at some of the smaller film festivals. I venture to suggest that in these days there are no small jobs or small festivals, but only small people. Hollywood could well pay more attention to our representation at international events.

I am not here to tell you what picture to make or not make, export or not export. I am here mainly to suggest that you take into account another dimension not normally present in the moviemaking process. That dimension is simply this: In a time when pressure is paramount and our way of life is in peril, how can I best serve my country and my people?

We are not asking you to surrender the prerogatives of the free press to cover any aspect of America that you choose. We are not asking you to load your guns in favor of this Administration. But we are asking you to deal in truth with yourselves and your country's future, and to realize that what you do will be seen, absorbed, and felt by millions of people the world over.

You people have chosen to work in Hollywood. By the nature of what you do, this makes you citizens of not only the United States but of the world.

It is this peculiar combination of history, destiny, and scrutiny that imposes these unusual burdens upon us—upon you and your colleagues as well as upon me and my agency. To you and the private sector of endeavor, it may be unfair. But it is also inescapable.

We live in a world we did not make. We are beset with burdens we did not seek. We all of us have an obligation to pay our debts to humanity and to our heritage. If we choose not to meet those obligations, then history will be the collector.

But the issue, I suggest, is not if we can afford to make the effort. The issue is how do we go about it.

5. The Lincoln Group of D.C., February 10, 1962

As I would not be a slave, so I would not be a master. This expresses my idea of democracy.
    Abraham Lincoln

The Lincoln Group of the District of Columbia[123] was founded in 1935 as an organization of members who love American history generally and the sixteenth president of the United States in particular. Mr. Murrow's acceptance to speak before this historical association is reflective of his love of America's greatest president, a president about whom every child in the United States has at least anecdotal knowledge. It gave Murrow an opportunity to relate Lincoln's efforts toward a "more perfect Union" to U.S.I.A. efforts to inspire and persuade foreign populations to America's strivings today.

This Lincoln Group of Lincolnphiles before whom Murrow spoke is not to be confused with the Lincoln Group in Washington that was founded in 1999 as a political intelligence organization. The latter company led private contractor propaganda efforts in Iraq on behalf of the George W. Bush administration, including paying Iraqi journalists to write favorable stories about the U.S. effort in Iraq as well as paying Sunni Muslim religious scholars to assist the U.S. military in promoting national elections and reducing Sunni support for insurgents.[124] This more recent Lincoln Group received much critical press for its payola efforts to persuade in Iraq, which undoubtedly any Murrow admirer would find antithetical to telling America's story about free speech and free press in emerging democracies.

Murrow's main point of emphasis in the following speech is that when it comes to America's efforts to persuade, the whole world is watching. Unlike the Soviet Union's closed society, this open society promotes self-government and a revolutionary spirit based on its founding. The United States of America was still under two hundred years, very young by global standards, but its measure of influence was old:

Our revolutionary documents are read and quoted worldwide. One of our small libraries in Africa had more requests for the Federalist Papers in a period of four weeks than the New York Public Library had in the course of a full year. Demonstrators rioting in another African land quoted in explanation of their conduct a passage from Thomas Jefferson. When Libya convened its Constitutional Convention our Agency furnished on request a copy of the U.S. Constitution to every member of the constitutional assembly, all of course translated into Arabic.

Murrow, like Lincoln, understood that battles are won in the field and not at headquarters. Pennsylvania Avenue could only do so much. (In Murrow's time, U.S.I.A. was located at 1776 Pennsylvania Avenue, two blocks from 1600 Pennsylvania Avenue.) What was needed was leadership among the public affairs and public diplomacy officers of his agency who could better explain what democracy in action looks like. 1962 was the 100th Anniversary of the Emancipation Proclamation, a document to which the 1,400 Foreign Service Officers of U.S.I.A. would turn in their efforts to influence the brotherhood of nations in Africa. Those efforts would be challenging as Africa and the rest of the world saw the struggle for equality taking place in the city bus, lunch counter, public restroom, and public university of the American South.

Murrow's Lincoln Group speech is a time capsule in several ways. He uses the vernacular "Negro" to refer to African Americans. This term was widely used in the 1960s, even as a point of identification by Martin Luther King, Jr. in his 1963 "I Have a Dream" speech. He also uses the words, "This I Believe," words made famous by Murrow in 1951 when he started a radio program by that name that featured "the living philosophies of thoughtful men and women of inspiration presented in the hope they may strengthen your beliefs so that your lives may be richer, fuller, happier."[125]

> This I believe deeply: There is no land where change so far reaching and so affecting the body politic could take

place in an atmosphere so free of frenzy. It is a measure
of the strength of a people that we do what we must do
in a way that comforts the conscience of people with
opposing points of view.

Murrow is referring to the struggle of African American minorities to reach equal protection under the law and a level of respect and dignity that a democratic republic promised from the time of Lincoln to the time of Kennedy. It was an imperfect struggle, as we all know, but Murrow's speech as USIA Director to a group of Lincoln followers underscores the value that the propaganda agency placed on reconciling America's ideals with its actions.

Edward R. Murrow
Lincoln Group of D.C.
Willard Hotel
Washington, D.C.
Saturday, February 10, 1962

Mr. Toastmaster Sir, Distinguished Guests, Ladies and Gentlemen. I trust it will not be deemed inappropriate if I deplore the absence of the plates, while at the same time expressing the hope that this state of affairs did not come about as a result of your committee on arrangements reading the advanced text of my remarks and deciding that the plates were not for throwing.

Should any of you have difficulty hearing this not all-together trepid voice, I pray you remain silent, lest you, Mr. Toastmaster, have the experience that befell a Toastmaster in London. When the speaker had droned on for many minutes to no particular purpose and had lost his audience, at which point a little man in the rear of the room rose and said, "Mr. Toastmaster, I cannot understand a single word the speaker is saying." At which point, the Toastmaster rose, bowed graciously, and said, "I shall be delighted to change places with you."

Gratitude, we are often told, is that measure of appreciation a man expresses for favors or benefits received. I am indeed grateful for your invitation this evening. And yet gratitude alone seems altogether inappropriate. For I have come not so much to share thoughts about Lincoln as to participate in the veneration of a legend. And legends, my friends, are not easily approached by mere mortals such as we.

I come as an interloper in the shrine of Lincolnesque recollection. There are, in this audience tonight, experts of Lincolnia with credentials far better than mine. I note that in times gone by your speakers have included such eminences as Allan Nevins, Bruce Catton, and Carl Sandburg. I know them all. They are scholars, historians, poets of the past. I am but a poor past broadcaster, a smatterer, who was privileged to use his limited talent on an unlimited medium, and who has chosen now to seek his daily bread in the public instead of the private arena. What novice new come to Lincoln could hope to improve on these phrases of Sandburg describing Lincoln as a man "…who is both steel and velvet, who is as hard as rock and soft as drifting fog, who holds in his heart and mind the paradox of terrible storm and peace unspeakable and perfect."

One century has passed and the paradox of storm and peace is still upon our land. Daily the communications pour in from around the globe, relating the difficulties and the doldrums of threatened interests. Not too different, perhaps, from the cables that poured in on Lincoln from the front, relating the dread and the disappointments of secession defended. I well recall one cable said to have arrived at the White House with the signature, "General Hooker. Headquarters, in the saddle." A day passed, and another came with the same signature: "General Hooker. Headquarters, in the saddle." It was on the third such cable's arrival that Lincoln is reported to have remarked wryly: "General Hooker has his headquarters where his hindquarters ought to be."

As you may know, I head an information agency with over 200 posts in 99 countries. Our headquarters are thus in the field where our 1,400 foreign service officers occupy our version of the front lines. The hindquarters are back here where I work in Washington.

I have just returned from a visit to part of those headquarters—two weeks ago I was in Africa. For most of the month of January I saw the fulminations of freedom that are welling up in those lands, I saw the anxious faces and eager hands of black men reaching for their future, I heard the voices and sounds of a tomorrow being spawned in the toil of today. I felt the thrill of excitement filling the hearts of these new men of Africa. These lands will never see their past again.

Their voice and their dream is the ebb tide on which history flows. And as the sea's ebb tide is relentless and unceasing, so too is the ebb tide which carries their dream through these days in which we now live.

There is in this, I suggest, an intense relevancy, for us who revere the memory of Abraham Lincoln. If there was any one man who could shape the destiny of a land and a people for generations to follow, surely it was Lincoln. Forging the bonds of insoluble national union, molding the course of nation building, leading his people into and out of chaotic struggle in which much was given, more was demanded, and all was committed, with blood strife their legacy, but nationhood their future. This was Lincoln, of course. But this, I suggest, is also Africa.

Here then is one full factor that puts this country in league with the "Revolution of Bright Hope" that is rising on our globe. We have a birthright on revolution. We are, in Henry Steele Commager's happy phrase, the oldest of the new nations, the first to be made out of an old world colony, ours the oldest written Constitution, the oldest continuous federal system and ours the oldest practice of self-government of any nation. And it is as a great revolutionary power that much of the world knows us.

Our revolutionary documents are read and quoted worldwide. One of our small libraries in Africa had more requests for the Federalist Papers in a period of four weeks than the New York Public Library had in the course of a full year. Demonstrators rioting in another African land quoted in explanation of their conduct a passage from Thomas Jefferson. When Libya convened its Constitutional Convention our Agency furnished on request a copy of the U.S. Constitution to every member of the constitutional assembly, all of course translated into Arabic. Without exaggeration, that shot fired "by the rude bridge that arched the flood" has been quite literally heard round the world. And its echoes continue to reverberate across lands like those I visited in Africa.

Lincoln fits into this picture more aptly than most. He does so because of his highly personal "legend of the leader."

Though born amid revolution, America was governed by aristocrats. George Washington, John Adams, Tom Jefferson, James Madison, James Monroe, John Quincy Adams—these were all educated men of letters, aristocrats of breeding and bearing. The southerners among them even held slaves. It was not until Andrew Jackson that a man "from the people" rose to the White House. But surely the most dramatized man of the people was Abe Lincoln. From log cabin to the Presidency, from rail splitter to nation builder, from common man to the leader of men. This was the legendary route of Lincoln, and it is the legend of the leadership about this country that is popularized abroad.

"Lincoln," said Woodrow Wilson, "owed nothing to his birth and everything to his growth." This was the path of Lincoln. This, I suggest, is also the path of Africa.

Lincoln is justly celebrated as the man who kept a nation from rending itself asunder. But if this was his canvas, his theme was larger. The effort was not only to preserve the union but to preserve for the world the most successful experiment in free government that history had yet seen. Many of you will remember that he said in his first message to Congress in July of 1861:

> "...it is a struggle for maintaining in the world that form and substance of government whose leading object is to elevate the condition of men--to lift artificial weights from all shoulders--to clear the paths of laudable pursuit for all--to afford all an unfettered start and a fair chance in the race of life."

Free men everywhere, he insisted, had a stake in the preservation of the Union, for the Union was "the last best hope of earth."

As early as the debates with Douglas, Lincoln propounded his doctrine of freedom for all. He declared that the men in Independence Hall were speaking to the whole world of men when they enunciated their principles.

> They reached forward and seized upon the farthest posterity. They erected a beacon to guide their children and their children's children…they established these great self-evident truths that when in the distant future some man, some faction, some interest, should set up the doctrine that none but rich men, or none but white men, were entitled to life, liberty and the pursuit of happiness, their posterity might look up again to the Declaration of Independence and take courage to renew the battle which their fathers began.

Americans were, in Lincoln's words, "God's Almost chosen people." A civil war, then, engaged not for our land alone but for whatever land the fortunes of history might some day smile upon.

Of equal relevance for emerging nations today is the very time in which Lincoln lived. The milieu of Lincoln was the milieu of the frontier, of a nation on the move, of the growing pains that marked its evolution from a primitive to a developing society. Lincoln over a century ago lived amid circumstances ideally duplicated in Africa today.

Note these words: "New nations would be carved out of old empires, fabulous new lands would be explored and opened up for human settlement, and new struggles for human freedom would be won. The old, slow-moving, horse-drawn and wind propelled modes of travel would give way to the (new)." R. Gerald McMurty wrote that. He was describing the America of Lincoln's day. He could as well have been describing the Africa of our day.

Amid the difficulties of burgeoning nationhood and a pain-wracked Civil War that near prostrated the republic, Lincoln proved himself a man of mighty principle. Lincoln had every reason to postpone the elections of 1864—the bloody war was in its fourth year, he had no assurance of his own re-election. But hold the election he did. Listen to his words writ large on the pages of history one week after the election: "...the election was a necessity. We cannot have free government without elections; and if the rebellion could force us to forgo, or postpone a national election, it might fairly claim to have conquered and ruined us....What has occurred in this case must ever recur in similar cases...the election, along with its incidental and undesirable strife, has done good too. It has demonstrated that a people's government can sustain a national election in the midst of a great civil war. Until now, it has not been known to the world that this was a possibility."

But it was a possibility. And the world saw it proven so. There may lie in this a moral for the newly arrived brotherhood of nations in Africa. We do not expect them to imitate our forms. On the contrary, contemplation of our Civil War should make us tolerant of the difficulties of other lands. Our own forms were roughhewn for us. Into them our people have poured their blood, their toil, their work, and their worry. These forms even today undergo constant change and adjustment. Why, then, should we feel that our way is the best way for other peoples as well? Discovering one's own path in one's own manner is part of the soil in which our rootholds have grown. As we would not deny it to ourselves, so should we not deny it to others.

But we do expect these other lands to be true to their own principles and practices. The lesson of Lincoln and the 1864 election amid the travail of Civil War is a lesson ignored by others only to their loss. It says, it seems to me, that the way of the expedient and the easy is not the way of the strong. This too is part of the "legend of the leader" that is Lincoln.

We celebrate this year the 100th Anniversary of the Emancipation Proclamation. In a time when local problems have become global concerns it seems prophetic that this epic pronunciamento on domestic freedom had foreign policy overtones as well. By making the extirpation of slavery one of the main objects of the war, Lincoln rallied the moral sense of England and France to his side. Britain and France could then only be unshakably for the Union. There was a tide of events running in the affairs of men even then.

One century later, the issue to which that proclamation was directed is still not at rest. The Negro has gained his freedom. He is still en route to gaining his equality.

The Proclamation resulted in political emancipation. Psychological emancipation has been longer coming. And the very nature of the Civil War has made its solution a difficult one. But because the War was severe, problems arising from it are of course severe. The south still has its bitter memories. Regional feeling and unity are still greater there than elsewhere in this country. And what more natural target for such lingering resentments than the very group which contributed a major issue to that fratricidal struggle, the Negro?

The most important aspect of slavery to impress itself on my mind is that it was NEGRO slavery. It was designed to regulate the relationships between black and white. The Civil War and the 13th Amendment changed the status of the Negro, but the economic and social relationships of black and white were not greatly changed. Justifications of slavery before the war could be applied with equal force and relevance after the war to support continuation of the Negro as a subordinate. Indeed, in our southland and my homeland today there are phrases uttered that but for the accident of time could be relevant to the issues bound up in the Civil War. This is not to say there is here a pro-slavery sentiment in the 20th century. Certainly not. Quite the contrary. But it does suggest that underlying the issues of slavery was a relationship of status between black and white. The nation one century later is still engrossed in realigning that relationship.

But the change of that relationship is inevitably stamped on the events of our day. Under Franklin Roosevelt Negro advisers were appointed to the Cabinet. Under Harry Truman the seal of the President's office was implanted upon the report of his Civil Rights Commission officially decrying the rights denied Negroes. In the 1950s there issued a Supreme Court decision that may well rank as the 20th Century Emancipation Proclamation—Brown vs. Board of Education, pronouncing separate facilities as inherently unequal. And only last month John F. Kennedy announced his intention of appointing the first Negro to sit in the President's Cabinet.

The Negro has come a long way in this land. He will go further. This country is indeed dedicated to the proposition that equality in the eyes of the law is not predicated upon color in the eyes of the beholder. This will take time because this land is equally dedicated to the rights and privileges of all its citizens. To change a majority, one respects a minority. And it will take place peacefully because this land is rooted in the soil of democracy and calm transition.

This I believe deeply: There is no land where change so far reaching and so affecting the body politic could take place in an atmosphere so free of frenzy. It is a measure of the strength of a people that we do what we must do in a way that comforts the conscience of people with opposing points of view.

Saul Padover recently authored a book called "The Genius of America." His chapter headings list the molders of the country as they seem to him best to be known: The American as Democrat: Thomas Jefferson. The American as Conservative: Alexander Hamilton. The American as Republican: James Madison. The American as Federalist: John Marshall. The American as Philosopher: Ralph Waldo Emerson. I could not help but note this chapter with a simpler listing: The American: Abraham Lincoln.

Perhaps that is how we best remember Lincoln—simply, the American.

Padover again says that America's most original contribution to political theory has been to have no theory. If true this be, then surely the capstone of our nationhood has been its people. If the American Dream were to be summed up in the figure of but one solitary person, surely that person would be the solemn Lincoln.

There was about him that most peculiar quality of manhood that history best calls destiny. In him was wrapped not the hope of one people but the dream of all peoples. The Civil War was fought not only to unify this nation or to free its slaves but for the freedom of men everywhere. Lincoln's life span of 56 years, 2 months, and 4 days is yet to end. And it may never, so long as men dare to tempt their dreams with the fervor of their hope.

His was a newborn age. He came into the world while Tom Jefferson was concluding his 8th year of the Presidency, that very winter that was the time of James Madison's inauguration and Bonaparte's invasion of Spain. A half-century later he would be the first President born beyond the confines of the 13 original states, even as one century later, John F. Kennedy would be the first President born in this century.

And in this land of ours—born in revolution, tempered in struggle, united in blood, nurtured amid hope, and seasoned with responsibility, the rising nations of Africa see more than just history alone. They would elevate their gaze to a horizon but dimly perceived by some but a horizon to which all of us are inevitably bound. To some it may seem they are caught in the pathological fervor of their nationalism. But I suggest that what we witness is but a fervent profile of what, but for the grace of the past two centuries, would be the early spawning of our own land of America.

6. American Management Association, February 16, 1962

History suggests that capitalism is a necessary condition for political freedom.
    Milton Friedman

1962 was the year of the publication of one of the most important books of the age, Milton Friedman's *Capitalism and Freedom*. Friedman takes issue with President John F. Kennedy's inaugural remarks, "Ask not what your country can do for you—ask what you can do for your country."

> The free man will ask neither what his country can do for him nor what he can do for his country. He will ask rather "What can I and my compatriots do through government" to help us discharge our individual responsibilities, to achieve our several goals and purposes, and above all, to protect our freedom? And he will accompany this question with another: How can we keep the government we create from becoming a Frankenstein that will destroy the very freedom we establish it to protect? Freedom is a rare and delicate plant. Our minds tell us, and history confirms, that the great threat to freedom is the concentration of power. Government is necessary to preserve our freedom, it is an instrument through which we can exercise our freedom; yet by concentrating power in political hands, it is also a threat to freedom. Even though the men who wield this power initially be of good will and even though they be not corrupted by the power they exercise, the power will both attract and form men of a different stamp.[126]

Notwithstanding Friedman's criticism of big government, the Kennedy administration was accommodating to business interests in the service of America's confrontation with the Soviet Union. His Democratic administration had not been elected with a majority mandate for progressive reforms in American capitalist policies. He was a practical liberal, not a leftist.

The foreign policies of the Kennedy administration are subject today to various interpretations about his level of activism and success, given the unfinished nature of JFK's term in office. He made colossal mistakes (Bay of Pigs, Diem Coup) and had heroic achievements (Nuclear Test Ban Treaty, Berlin speech, Cuban Missile Crisis). He was much more foreign policy directed than some other American presidents, having once said, "Domestic policy can only defeat us; foreign policy can kill us." His 1961 Inaugural Address is completely bereft of any domestic policy concerns or problems, including race relations. Instead, he called on a new 1960s generation of young idealist Americans to serve their country and to defend freedom abroad "in its hour of maximum danger." His administration was very much directed toward restoring America' image in the world through various methods—economic, social, and military. This explains his support for counterinsurgency tactics in Southeast Asia, in part due to his reaction to Soviet Premier Nikita Khrushchev's call for Soviet support of wars of national liberation.

His administration, focused as it was so much on the Cold War, championed the forces of democratic capitalism in the contested regions of the Third World, most notably Africa, Latin America, and Southeast Asia. Kennedy's Alliance for Progress with 22 nations of Latin America was designed to promote greater economic ties and social and economic reforms in the Northern Hemisphere. It is not considered a great success, but it holds up symbolically as a program that advanced Kennedy's international popularity.

Edward R. Murrow's speech before the American Management Association illustrates what the United States Information Agency is doing in its promotion of American capitalism over Soviet communism. It is an example of how the Agency was utilized in the service of American commercial and corporate agendas overseas. One of the most requested economic volumes overseas in 1962, according to Murrow, is USA: The Permanent Revolution, based on a 1951 special issue of Fortune magazine. It touts a very favorable view of

American business interests in protecting the worker and forging more efficiency and equality.

It's important to recognize the Murrow's audience that day represented big business in America. These were not mom and pop operators but rather the Fortune 500 types gathered to hear a former famous journalist turned government propagandist explain how the federal government was in concert with the goals of industry:

> Let me take one subject and show you how my Agency responds. It is a subject, incidentally, designed to appeal to, among other audiences, foreign workers. It is the subject of the American economy. How do we explain our brand of capitalism abroad, particularly when so many people have been indoctrinated with the concept that ours remains an 18th century capitalism?

The 1960s was a decade of enormous growth in per capita output and income. A majority of Americans was earning a middle-class income. Big business was no enemy as it is often viewed today. It was an age of affluence and though we often think of "gaps" associated with the Kennedy years—missile, education, race, or space—the optimism associated with Kennedy and his "best and brightest" advisers is palpable in this speech. Murrow asks his listeners, as his boss asked of his fellow Americans in 1961, to join forces, business with government, since both sectors had a common pursuit. "It is in pursuit of common goals from common concerns that we ask you to join us—simply the defense of free men everywhere."

Edward R. Murrow
American Management Association
Annual Meeting
Palmer House Hilton, Chicago
February 16, 1962

Ladies and gentlemen, you will appreciate I am sure that this is a difficult assignment for a bureaucrat just ending the first year of his sentence, sort of the Satchel Paige of this administration.

Upon entering this hotel, I was reminded of my days as a reporter by noticing that Xavier Cugat is performing in this hostelry, and I recalled that his wife several years ago confided to me that she was coming down the elevator in a hotel in Las Vegas and heard one lady say to another, "Who is that man who is playing here, that Excalibur Catgut they call him?"

When I first undertook this assignment, I went to see a friend of mine, Senator Dick Russell, and at the end of the conversation he said to me, "Well, this is a tough job you've undertaken and there will be times when you will feel like a cat licking the grindstone."

It is with real diffidence that I raise this abrasive voice with such distinguished company, a voice which was once described in all candor by an old and good friend as being a combination of a whiskey baritone and an unfrocked bishop.

But I shall like to talk to you briefly about the Agency I head. It has no constituency. It reports directly to the president, receives its appropriations from Congress. Its work begins at the water's edge. What we do therefore is invisible, the results frequently intangible, and we manage to receive public notice when we fall on our face, of which upon occasion we do.

I am recently returned from Africa. I saw there with my own eyes the excitement and exhilaration of peoples anxious to leap into the second half of the 20th century, ready or not. As for themselves, theirs is the legacy of hope after decades of dormancy. As for us, ours is the legacy of challenge after decades of neglect.

You have convened for what I am told is your mid-winter personnel conference. May I commend your concern and relate to you that we are partners in our anxiety over personnel. In my wanderings around West Africa few things impressed me more than that sometimes happy coincidence of the right man, in the right place, on the right job. The equation of personnel ambition corresponding to work challenge is as delicate as the human chemistry upon which it depends. There are instances in Africa when we have had the good fortune to solve that equation, and it is then exciting indeed to see a man involved in his work who in his work involves the men whom he daily contacts.

It was in Ghana, near the capital city of Accra, that I had my first experience with a "Mammy Wagon." A Mammy Wagon could properly be described as a converted-like truck with wooden benches into which there is crammed human beings, goats, chickens, bags of peanuts. They are always overloaded and they carry slogans in English, slogans such as "God is good," "lonely boy," "I shall return," "He who does bad hurts himself." But the one that appealed to me most is one that came close to stating man's modern dilemma. It read quite simply, "The Lord is my shepherd—I know not why."

So that peoples abroad cannot make the same complaint of not knowing about the United States is the reason for being of my Agency.

We are in pursuit of men's minds and opinions. It is an elusive goal. You do not win them quickly or easily. Once won, they give you no commitment that they will stay won. They are people like you and me. They will change their minds as capriciously or as often as we do. They will judge us more by what we do than by what we say. A Cuban invasion can defame the name of this country in Latin America, just as an Alliance for Progress can do much to honor it.

Let me take one subject and show you how my Agency responds. It is a subject, incidentally, designed to appeal to, among other audiences, foreign workers. It is the subject of the American economy. How do we explain our brand of capitalism abroad, particularly when so many people have been indoctrinated with the concept that ours remains an 18th century capitalism?

Our television service has been able to inject the concepts and values of free enterprise and private ownership into many overseas programs. Beginning in 1956 we distributed the "Industry on Parade" series worldwide, produced by the National Association of Manufacturers and describing the high productivity, versatility and technical know-how of American industry. Worldwide distribution also went to

"Americans at Work," produced by the AFL-CIO, illustrating the role played by free labor in our capitalist system.

Individual programs in the worldwide "Assignment USA" series treated American capitalism. A show called "Small Business" described the concept of private ownership, initiative and drive. "The Education of Johnny Schnell" illustrated private ownership and initiative by describing such incidents as a boy's paper route, and his father's job with the telephone company where, as one of its employees, he owned stock as well as receiving a salary.

Our "Report from America" series in many language versions has depicted topics such as leisure time, supermarkets, farming, homebuilding, shopping centers, suburban families, public schools, small farms, household appliances, motels, and summer theaters—all reflecting our private enterprise system.

Our broadcasts have emphasized that peaceful cooperation between labor and management in this country has displaced class conflict. Representatives of the Voice of America regularly cover meetings of economists and businessmen, such as this meeting of the American Management Association. We've carried series on the history of capitalism, on economic crises, on the role of the stock exchange, and on sources of economic growth.

We've done series on big American corporations such as the Dow Chemical Company, the DuPont Company, American Telephone and Telegraph, The Atlantic and Pacific, the Travelers Insurance Company, The Story of Oil, The Story of Coal, and others. Our latest program involved the operations of Armco International in 23 countries and the benefits derived by nations where this firm does business.

Our press service turns out pamphlets, columns, and news articles that get printed the world around. Note this sampling of the type of material featured: an article emphasizing the vitality of our system through the nation's progress in space research and exploration and the promise of greater things to come, at the same time illustrating the essentially civilian character of American society; another notes the strength of the US economy compared to that of the USSR, showing the basic differences in approach and philosophy and the growing ability of our system to meet the needs and aspirations of the people as against the Soviet system.

Our press people have also distributed some interesting picture layouts—like the one called "Lunchbox Capitalists," showing steelworkers reading the Wall Street Journal on their lunch hour to check on the stocks in their own company that they have bought, or a Negro steelworker who received a letter from his company president offering him stock options under a bonus plan. Or another layout entitled "Meet an American Ditch Digger," the story of Bill McVey, a guy who owns his own tractor, revels in being his own boss, does excavating and ditch work for people around Aurora, Missouri, and then returns to the close-knit family life of his wife and four kids.

In our overseas translation program, which has run to over 60,000,000 copies, the first and second all-time most published titles are two vigorous defenses of American capitalism: The Big Change by Frederick Lewis Allen and Capitalism in America by Frederick Stern. Another much demanded volume has been USA: The Permanent Revolution by the editors of Fortune. Taken together, these three books alone account for 80 foreign language printings. And in West Africa today, one of the hottest items in our library happens to be The Federalist Papers. Indeed, in one small post in Africa, we recorded in a period of weeks more requests for The Federalist Papers than was recorded by the New York Public Library, the second largest in the country, in the course of an entire year.

We have also produced in translation, Private Investment: Key To International Industrial Development by James Daniel. An American, after ordering copies for his company's foreign employees, took a copy to read on the plane leaving Honduras. His seat companion, upon noticing the title of the book, stopped reading his own paperback detective novel and began reading over the American's shoulder. The American asked him if he would like to browse through the book for the rest of the flight. The stranger accepted. When the plane landed in

Guatemala, the stranger expressed his sorrow at being unable to read the book more closely, whereupon the American offered to let him keep the volume. The stranger accepted and introduced himself as Vice-Minister of Economy for Nicaragua, en route to a meeting of the Central American Commodity Market, where he felt this book, produced in translation by our Agency on private industrial development, would be useful to him.

We have over a dozen exhibits currently showing abroad on the subject of the U.S. Economic System. Here are a few examples: A New American Family—showing the rapid adjustment of a Hungarian refugee family to life in our free enterprise society. A Progressive Economy—showing how Americans have achieved the highest standard of living in the world by means of a free enterprise system, disproving the Marxian prediction that under capitalism the rich would get richer and the poor poorer. How Americans Earn Their Living—defining the content and characteristics of the U.S. labor force, showing methods and techniques that make it skilled and productive.

We have also had this year traveling throughout the Soviet Union three exhibits: one dealing with plastics, one dealing with transportation in this country, and a third just leaving, dealing with medicine. These exhibits are handled by twenty to twenty-five Russian-speaking American guides. They will be visited each day by 9, 10, 12 thousand Russians. Much of the questioning has to do—not with the exhibit—but the Russians, who have an abiding curiosity about this country, will come up and say, "How much did that suit cost you?" "How many hours did you have to work to own it?" "Do unemployed get compensation in the United States?" "Is the American worker permitted to strike?" This means a direct communication, which satisfies to a degree and also raises certain doubts in the minds of the Russian visitors.

It would be churlish of me to come here without acknowledging the contribution that American industry has made to these and other exhibits, because we do not have funds to go out and purchase the items to be exhibited. Therefore, we scrounge and we ask American industries to provide items for the exhibit. And in all three of those that I have mentioned, we have probably had from 150 to 200 thousand dollars of material provided to the government by private industry in this country.

All of this I have mentioned illustrates a phase in our Agency's work in the field of economics. Many of the examples are oriented to facets of life and labor in this country about which foreign working people would be curious. It is a trying task to describe something as enormously complex as the American economy to non-industrialized societies. Many of them have no remotely comparable experience and find it difficult to understand some of what is told them. Some of them do not even have a language capable of dealing with the subject. But it is a task in which I feel this Agency has had some degree of success.

If the "Worker In Other Countries" is your concern, then I must report to you a new direction this Agency is taking. It is a labor information program. Nine labor information specialists are being assigned in Latin America to Argentina, Venezuela, Bolivia, Peru, Mexico, Uruguay, Colombia, Brazil, and Chile.

Their job is an important one, for labor is a vital objective, both for ourselves and the Communists. It is the Latin American worker, in farm and factory, who possesses, in President Kennedy's words, the "unsatisfied aspirations for economic progress and social justice." And it is to the worker that Communism, if it is to triumph in this hemisphere, must prove its case and gain its victory. That is why, if the Latin American worker is not be lost to the cause of freedom, our response in Latin America must be as bold and as big as is the challenge we confront.

These labor information officers will work closely with local workers and their groups. They will encourage democratic workers' organizations and improvement of workers' living standards. They will stress the advantage of cooperation with democratic parties rather than with Castro–Communist movements. They will inform the more advanced trade unions about the basics of free democratic trade unionism—such as organization, collective bargaining, grievance procedures, community responsibility.

They will expose the false claim of Communism to champion the world's workers. They will show Communism in its true light as exploiter of the working class. They will combat Communist infiltration of free labor unions and demonstrate that Communism is an international conspiracy against personal and national freedom working through captive labor movements to impose Communist world domination.

To do this, they will use a variety of methods: labor newspapers, labor radio shows, pamphlet programs, films, movies, books, education centers, seminars, and the exchange of persons program. All of this, of course, only supplements the most important element of all: the individual labor specialist himself, engaging in vital face-to-face confrontation in those places and with those persons to whom his appeal is addressed.

I am not so naïve as to suggest that what this Agency does can win the world. But I am honest enough to acknowledge that quite spectacular results can be achieved. In Pakistan, for example, a strike in a local factory threatened unemployment for the workers in the area. The strike was avoided, and the local authorities give credit for this to a most non-economic factor: one of our films called "Union Local." Despite pressures from leftist leaders of the union to go on strike, the majority of workers decided that if workers in the United States could settle grievances through negotiations, they should make the same attempt. They had seen the movie and the strike failed.

If a single film could do this, imagine what one man full-time with the resources of a program at his command might hope to accomplish.

This concerted effort on labor that I mentioned in Latin America is part of my Agency's role in the Alliance for Progress.

It is in this context of the kind of war we are in that American business firms responded to the overseas information program I mentioned last November in Houston. There I stated that we were cooperating with

150 firms to supply material on crucial issues to their overseas American representatives from home offices. In the 13 weeks since then, more than 180 additional firms have offered their cooperation. We estimate some 4,500 American business representatives abroad have been asked by their companies to study material on foreign policy issues. Thus when our overseas businessman discusses world affairs, particularly those issues in which America has a major stake, he speaks from greater knowledge. His conversation, without parroting the government line, can be a very helpful influence on his foreign friends, frequently people of very considerable importance and influence in their own community. Frequently, too, these associates are quite different from the official American diplomatic community.

The business world's response indicates that most firms are convinced that the Alliance for Progress must succeed if Latin America is going to remain in the Free World. If your own firms have representatives in Latin America or elsewhere overseas, and we have not asked for your help, we would appreciate hearing from you.

I think I bandy no empty emphasis when I suggest this thought: We cannot allow the Alliance to fail. Announced almost a year ago by President Kennedy, it is free society's response to poverty and pestilence, to ignorance and indolence. Should these efforts of free men fail, the lusty shouting in the offstage wings of Latin America by Castro and his cohorts would herald the inevitability that their solutions will be tried. The history of our day has recorded part of the price for the Castro-type solution. It has also recorded, how difficult it is to remove such actors from the stage.

It is in pursuit of common goals from common concerns that we ask you to join us—simply the defense of free men everywhere. As one of my colleagues is wont to say: The Cold War water is fine. Come on in.

7. National Association of Broadcasters, March 2, 1962

True wisdom is less presuming than folly. The wise man doubteth often, and changeth his mind; the fool is obstinate, and doubteth not; he knoweth all things but his own ignorance.
   Akhenaton

In many respects the following speech by Murrow before the National Association of Broadcasters brings his career full circle, and not just because he is before his former industry compatriots. Rather, he is coming home to his need to teach. He was always a journalist first, but a journalist with a message. We all know our best teachers. They don't just instruct; they serve as life models of excellence. That was his Ida Lou Anderson. Murrow didn't just report. If that were all he did he would have been far less admired. He modeled excellence in broadcasting so that his peers and his hires would want to do their best. In wartime, he served as a collective conscience for a nation watching a war slowly make its way to its shores. It all began during the London Blitzkrieg from the roof of Broadcasting House, headquarters of the British Broadcasting Corporation. He had no sense of danger, just a desire to give a firsthand account of what it was like watching German bombers overhead or to interview Londoners in air raid shelters. The American people would change their opinion about this European war based on those broadcasts.

Is Murrow really as good as he is so mythologized? As times goes by, he holds up well as "the voice of history" as some have called him. He is credited with five thousand radio and television broadcasts and five Peabody awards (broadcast journalism's best). Honors abound for this journalist. But it is this Murrow, in failing health, who takes the "warts and all" approach to America's place in the world. This former king among knights said that a bit of soul-searching was in need. America was complacent. It often thought that just telling America's story was enough since our virtues seemed to outweigh anything else on offer. Americans have a Manichean view of the world—us versus them, but such thinking is outmoded in an age of NATO, the United Nations, the Organization of American States.

> Difficult problems will only surrender to difficult solutions. Some problems may have no immediate solution at all. Our conception of right and wrong may not be right for the wrongs of others. The issues of the world are multi-sided and many varied. They may not all be settled in our favor.

Murrow is exercising a bit of practical magic. He is acknowledging that simple solutions will not work and won't come easy. This is not a message easily digested by American broadcast executives whose training and education is marinated in the First Amendment and the sacred legal protections of free speech and free press. Didn't this make the U.S. model of journalism the best model for the world? If one follows Murrow's line of reasoning here, the U.S. journalism model—much less its political culture—is not a natural and inevitable world model. The U.S. must accept that it holds no monopoly on the best way, however self-assured and confident it may feel.

This does not mean that there is no task at hand for these broadcasters. The Communist model "relies on the weapons of subversion, propaganda, infiltration, brute terror and naked force. But it has conspicuously failed. It has been frustrated by the United States, by its Allies, by the United Nations, by nations of other passions, and perhaps most of all by the determination that where men have the will to be free they will be free."

It is in this speech that Murrow lays out his USIA legacy: to free men's minds, not through indoctrination but through example:

> And I would suggest, in all seriousness, that how we conduct ourselves in this country, the type of society we fashion, the expansion of political, social, economic equality, decency and justice, may have much more to do with our case abroad, may be much more effective than the dollars we send abroad.

His approach was to have the United States, in all its shortcomings, act as a competitive model to the Soviet Union, particularly in the Third World countries where the USSR was gaining a foothold with its guerrilla insurgencies. In Africa alone, USIA increased its post presence almost three-fold (thirteen to thirty-three) in response to decolonization, though the efforts to persuade were always marred by any political setback and violence associated with the U.S. civil rights movement.[127]

Edward R. Murrow, Director, U.S. Information Agency
National Association of Broadcasters
Shoreham Hotel, Washington, D.C.
March 2, 1962

I must confess that today I feel like an old friend returned to home. Broadcasting, as you have been told, was once my daily bread. In a sense that is still true. But like many of you I now run an organization. And sometimes in the waning of those midmorning conferences I am wont to think back to the early days in broadcasting and the saga of that now perhaps immortal cub reporter sent to cover his first big story. It was the Jonestown flood. The height of the tragedy was fast approaching. The paper held out its lead beyond press time waiting for the cub's first reports, which finally arrived with the following cryptic message: "Chaos reigns. Nothing can be learned."

It is, I hope, true of my present work that chaos reigns rarely but that there is much to be learned. It is this, in part, that gives chilling dimension to much of what my Agency does. The stake in our deliberations is not the success or failure of a good show but the rise or fall of a free world interest. You translate your efforts into ratings gained, public acceptance, esteem and respect, or dollars lost. We translate ours into persons persuaded or diplomacy lost.

I must confess that I was tempted to talk today entirely about the work of this Agency, an independent agency reporting directly to the President, budget a hundred and a eleven point five million, using all known instruments of communication in an effort to tell the American story abroad. However I concluded that were I to do so, you would perhaps regard this as an unduly long commercial that profited you very little; therefore, I thought to talk in the line of your discussion this morning as perhaps a personal editorial on the state of this small but troubled planet.

There are great challenges afoot on this globe today. The Soviet has chosen to engage us in a type of fateful competition, testing whether free men still have the will to be free. There is, I suggest, a tendency in this country to drop the plumb line of measurement into our troubled diplomatic waters and calculate thereby the extent of our successes or failure: as of such a date, there are so many victories won, so many failures lost. Being a self-critical society, we chronicle the factors that some feel to go against us:

- a lingering suspicion in some new countries of Western colonialism and capitalism;
- long-range intellectual leanings toward socialism;
- envy in some countries of the purported economic progress achieved under Communism, with little recognition of the fact that Western progress serves as the goal to which all people, including the Russians, aspire;
- a desire in some lands to maximize foreign aid from both camps;
- and a basic naïveté about the realities of Communism.

I suggest we misread the signs. Some matters we consider negative may not in fact appear to be what they actually are. The counsel of despair for the cause of democracy is the counsel of the ignorant. It may be that we are a nation poorly prepared for our global role. But if poorly cast are we, then higher striving must there be.

We are, I think you would agree, a pragmatic people. We test the validity of propositions by their practical results. This was a pioneer land built by a pioneer people. To physical challenge we responded with physical strength.

I suggest we are set in our ways of our thinking, and it is a way ill conceived for the complexities of this day. Consider these considerations:

- From a history that has solved all problems we assume that if "problem" there be then "solution" we will find;
- From a history that has known little frustration we seek easy answers to difficult problems;
- From a history molded on the rightness of our national virtue we seem self-assured that things will naturally go our way. We feel we are right and we are American and the world will surely see the right of our American way if it is simply explained to them; we are, in a sense, only an explanation away from total victory;
- From a history that has simplified our troubles into terms of "we" and "they" we assume there are only two sides to any question—and not three or ten or 15 sides as there are in NATO, or 20 sides as there are in the Organization of American States, or 104 sides as there are in the United Nations;
- From a history that has taught us the value of "right" and "wrong" we leave no room for different descriptions of the same problem by different people. Thus Khrushchev calls Berlin a "bone in his throat" and a "cancer" while we term it a "showcase of freedom" and a "symbol of hope." Perhaps what is symbol to us is cancer to him, and that is exactly why it is a problem.

Thus do some of the enthrallments of our nationhood poorly cast us for the role we must now play…a role we did not seek. We're a good people. We are loath to use the whip, the knout, the fist and its force. It may well be that while we grew up as a land, the world of our growth changed beyond all dimension. Difficult problems will only surrender to difficult solutions. Some problems may have no immediate solution at all. Our conception of right and wrong may not be right for the wrongs of others. The issues of the world are multi-sided and many-varied. They may not all be settled in our favor. As George Bernard Shaw said, "Do you think the laws of God will be suspended in favor of this country because you were born in it?"

And it was the counsel of Abraham Lincoln that read: "We must disenthrall ourselves."

The fate of this land and this people will be decided by what we do on three fronts: the way we conduct ourselves here at home, the way we conduct ourselves confronting the Communist foe, the way we conduct ourselves in the vast arena of marginal lands with multiplying people.

Our conduct at home is a matter of our common concern. Our conduct regarding the Soviets is a matter of our common defense. Our conduct regarding the new nations is a matter of our common effort. How we regard them all in concert is a matter of our common destiny. I, for one, would not wish to prejudge the issue in any area.

But in this world of discomfiture where all of us live on the narrow margin between happiness and holocaust, it is well that we try to assess our position.

Communism came to power in Russia due to World War I. Communism came to power in China due to World War II. It has never come to power in any nation not disrupted by war, by civil war, or by both. It has never come to power but by the force of military might in being, in place, and without opposition. It has succeeded as a scavenger. It has failed as a leader.

The Communist Party of the Soviet Union is challenged both within and without its own world. These years have seen rebellion in Budapest, uprisings in Poland, revolts in East Germany, repression throughout the satellite empire. There is a wall in Berlin damming the flood tide of fleeing humanity. There is dissension in Peking and Tirana to add to that of Belgrade. Communist parties in Europe have shrunk drastically.

The Soviet Union, as a nation, is permanent come to the councils of world concern. But for the last decade its foreign policy has failed to expand its control. It relies on the weapons of subversion, propaganda, infiltration, brute terror and naked force. But it has conspicuously failed. It has been frustrated by the United States, by its Allies, by the United Nations, by nations of other passions, and perhaps most of all by the determination that where men have the will to be free they will be free.

The catalogue of Soviet difficulties is an impressive one:

> Their unity with China is increasingly in question.
>
> Communist parties throughout the world are doing less business.
>
> There has been little sale on their ideology.
>
> Neutrals will not be bought with guns and dams.
>
> Capitalism's amazing vigor runs counter to their dogma.
>
> The Alliance has not groaned but has grown.
>
> Western Europe rises to new union.
>
> The United Nations is slowly acquiring a capacity for world responsibility.

And in the words of Harlan Cleveland, the hard line boys in the Kremlin should be muttering about people who are "soft on capitalism."

This land can manage the difficult and demanding task of free alliance with other sovereign nations. This the Soviet Union cannot do.

This land can cooperate and accommodate and even compromise in the handling of global problems. This the Soviet seems unwilling to do.

This land can live with the Charter of the United Nations. This the Soviet cannot do.

This land can identify its legitimate national hopes with the national hopes of other nations. And this the Soviet cannot do.

Theirs is the way of orthodoxy. Theirs is the way of creed without deviation, the dogma without dissent, the conformity to which all must adhere. If theirs be the world of coercion, then ours is the world of free choice. To a globe now fumbling with new found freedoms, to lands now groping for their own place in the constellation of nations, this land, this people, has much to offer. A Communist, I suggest, cannot look upon the future with sanguine confidence.

But this struggle is now not near ended. It is not likely to be resolved quickly, easily, cleanly, or simply. If gains we have garnered there are still tasks to be tried.

And you, ladies and gentlemen, I venture to suggest, can share in this endeavor. I have suggested the three arenas where our fortunes lie: at home, against the Soviets, and in the new lands.

We must all of course join in the unfinished task of finishing the molding of our own land. This country was founded upon belief in great ideals. It is to the zealots that we owe our heritage—our belief in education, in social justice, in the living wage, in freedom of speech with the right of dissent and the critique of conformity, in all the importance of all men as equal and kindred souls. But these are subjects unknown in some places, and unwanted in others.

There are abroad on this planet great masses of people totally insulated from this country and what it believes only by the pall of their ignorance. It is the job of my Agency to try and reach these people. And reach them we will try. But the U.S. Information Agency can only be as effective in reaching men's minds as the society it serves. Desirable or not, we shall reflect what we are. If we would have the world think better of us, then we must better ourselves.

I would like to suggest that without speaking of running my Agency, this has in fact been a speech of how my Agency runs, because it can run in no other way.

For the USIA is the new dimension of the new diplomacy. We occupy the battle line that engages this entire land. We seek to explain this country and all it does. Our goal is the minds of men. But the war we wage is not to capture men's minds; it is a war to free them. And I would suggest, in all seriousness, that how we conduct ourselves in this country, the type of society we fashion, the expansion of political, social, economic equality, decency and justice, may have much more to do with our case abroad, may be much more effective than the dollars we send abroad.

The way of free men, as we all know, is the way of difficulty. If all may think, then all must be explained. If each may dissent, then each must be convinced.

We in the Agency must talk of full stomachs to those who have known only hunger. We must speak of comfortable lives to those who have known only toil. We must talk of the future and its dream to those who have known only the past and its despair. And we must speak of freedom to men who have known only subjection.

We must tell unfree men that freedom in some places may be a sometime thing. And to those newly free we must caution against having left one form of control only to deliver themselves to a new and heavier yoke. It is difficult and complex, this concept of freedom. But it is priceless, this dream we offer to share. And share it we must. And we shall know that in laboring for our children and ourselves, we labor in fact for all mankind. And all mankind will be in our debt, if we but realize that our heritage is the heritage of hope. For with our hopes go the fate of free men everywhere.

8. American Advertising Federation, June 19, 1963

The United States, as the world knows, will never start a war. We do not want a war. We do not now expect a war. This generation of Americans has already had enough—more than enough— of war and hate and oppression.
    John F. Kennedy, June 1963

In June 1963, Edward R. Murrow was continuing to display his frustration with Congress for not fully funding his influence agency. In this speech in Atlanta before the American advertising industry's largest membership organization, Murrow chastises the "vote of no confidence" from the House of Representatives.

He reports that the House had just approved $15 million less than the Agency had requested. Then he proceeds to lay out in detail what that $15 million propaganda gap means in terms of lost films, fewer information posts and reduced operating costs. He shares his hope to restore the cuts through the Senate, but throughout his tenure at USIA, his money woes put him on an endless rollercoaster ride. Overall, he left USIA with an increase in its budget, but not the kind of uptick one might expect from the most famous director in its history.

Budget worries and hat-in-hand requests to elected officials were never Murrow's forte, nor had the finance side at CBS been his comfort zone. He was always an ideas man more than a numbers cruncher, and he thought that good ideas should trump questions of costs.

To be so forthcoming with a public audience about the lack of Congressional appropriations was highly unusual for a government agency director. As a man whose entire career took place on a public stage, Murrow undoubtedly thought that he had both the stage and the duty. Though hamstrung by Congress as the sole source of annual funding for the United States Information Agency, he also thought that no one else besides him and perhaps his Deputy Director Donald M. Wilson could advocate with as much credibility. He knew that his reputation for honesty and integrity would fly high with this commercial advertising gathering, and given the likely attendance of many top executives from industry, he hoped that they would report his woes to their Congressional members in their home districts.

The propaganda gap with Soviets is reminiscent of President John F. Kennedy's missile gap thesis propounded when he was in the U.S. Senate and throughout his 1960 presidential campaign. Though Kennedy learned that the perceived gap was more fiction than fact, Murrow's propaganda gap was quite accurate. Walter Joyce points this out in his 1963 book, *The Propaganda Gap*:

> The USIA budget is less than General Motors spends to sell cars or Proctor & Gamble spends to sell soap. Because of its orphan status, it is a convenient whipping boy for congressional appropriations committees. Edward R. Murrow, latest in a string of USIA directors, was obviously appalled when his request for a modest increase in appropriations was met with rebuffs. Betraying a deep feeling of frustration before the House appropriations subcommittee, he blurted in 1961, "Sir, I must suggest, that the overall priority may not be in perspective. We are asking, if we receive our entire budget, for less than the cost of one Polaris submarine. If you consider our single appropriation measured against the Defense Department's appropriation, the Defense Department's appropriation for one year would run this agency for 400 years."[128]

Joyce identifies Representative John J. Rooney of Brooklyn, New York, as the "chief antagonist" of USIA. Rooney was chairman of the House subcommittee on appropriations during Murrow's tenure. Joyce describes Rooney as "a zealot over saving a dollar and a skeptic about the values of propaganda."

Stanley Silverman, who spent 47 years with the Agency and received a meritorious award under Murrow as Comptroller, told a similar story about Rooney's stranglehold over USIA appropriations. Silverman said, "When Edward R. Murrow was Director, he appeared before the Appropriations Committee to defend the Agency's budget request. He was clearly uncomfortable in that role, though the Democrats were in control of the House and Senate in those days and he was part of a Democratic administration. The Chairman of the House Appropriations subcommittee was Representative John J. Rooney of Brooklyn, who had been a District Attorney. He was antagonistic toward every bureaucrat who appeared before him, with the notable exception of J. Edgar Hoover. Hoover took pride in the fact that every year he would return part of his appropriations from Congress. The word was that he would make FBI agents work overtime without pay just to make sure he could turn back money to Appropriations." Silverman said that when Murrow had to face someone like Rooney, "you could see the tension in him. It wasn't nervousness, because he had been on the public stage for so long. He (Murrow) didn't get into the nuts and bolts. He didn't get into the nuts and bolts of the hearings; he didn't get into the nuts and bolts of the Agency's management either."[129]

Murrow's star status in the Kennedy administration may have actually hampered him in his appearances before Congress. Some may have resented his celebrity appeal, while others may have felt protected by Smith-Mundt Act restrictions that prohibited USIA from building up any domestic constituency that could lobby on its behalf. There were some great supporters at the time, namely Representative Dante Fascell (D-Florida), who, says Silverman, "became the patron saint of public diplomacy." Fascell was a champion of the third pillar in diplomacy: the ideological or psychological, to match the U.S. military and economic pillars of diplomacy. Fascell, like Murrow, believed that propaganda programs were not just tools of war but could be just as effective in peacetime engagement and help to overcome the propaganda gap with the Soviet Union.[130] Here Murrow is trying to make a connection between his sponsors—the American people—and his main client, the U.S.A., his most important client of his career.

Edward R. Murrow
American Advertising Federation

59th Convention
Atlanta, Georgia
June 19, 1963

It is good to be back in the company of advertising people. I remember the days when I had one, two, and sometimes three sponsors. Now I have 188 million. I suppose it might be appropriate at this late date to deny a particularly scurrilous rumor to the effect that I left the private sector of communication and entered government service because there was about to appear on television a program featuring a talking horse called Mr. Ed backed by a stable of excellent writers. Although candor compels me to confess that my government car provided by the taxpayers is in fact labeled Car 54 on the telephone system.

Our client is, of course, in advertising terms, the United States of America; more particularly it is the government of the United States acting in behalf of the people of this land. Our client demands and we owe him only our very best.

We are on the ground in 104 different countries. Some of these countries are directly opposed in varying degrees one to another—India and Pakistan, Israel and the Arab States, the Congo and South Africa. Yet we must operate in them all.

The message we convey is not a simple one. Ours is a land of multiple ideology. Democracy is not simple but complex. We allow, even encourage, dissent. Variety is our hallmark. We have made it a national credo not to have one belief, one rationale, one guide, one dogma. We have made a veritable dogma of having no dogma.

Thus it is that our Agency has been the recipient of great volumes of advice.

The political scientist, the professor, the student, the researcher, the sociologist, the psychologist, the anthropologist, the newspaperman, the broadcaster, the businessman, the sales manager, the missionary, and the writer—they all have answers to our questions in the business of propaganda. There are yet times when I feel that everyone in this country knows how to run this agency except me. But the very variety of source and suggestion is enough to suggest that no one person has a monopoly on the how of understanding the United States.

As a people, I suspect we prefer it this way. We would suspicion any man who suggests he has a monopoly on what to do or how to think or what to say. When someone comes forth to assert such, the American experience puts the lie to his assertion.

Our concern is with the idea and the ideal. We cannot gauge our success by sales. No profit and loss statement sums up our operations at the end of each year. No cash register rings when a man changes his mind. No totals are rung up on people impressed with an idea. There is no market listing of the rise or fall in the going rate of belief in an ideal. Often, one's best work may be merely to introduce doubt into minds already firmly committed. There are no tallies to total or sums to surmise when you've finished a day of explaining disarmament or discussing with the disenchanted the hope of an Alliance for Progress.

In short, our job is far different from selling a product to a single mass market. We are not selling America abroad for America is not for sale. Sloganeering and boasting of cars and washing machines is a product of the past. How much food and how many refrigerators we have in America is hardly a persuasive message to men who have no food either to refrigerate or to eat.

As you know, ours is an independent agency reporting directly to the President and receiving its budget through Congressional appropriations. We have no constituency, our work begins at the water's edge, our results are frequently intangible. We generally receive domestic publicity when we make a mistake, and that is as it should be. Our budget can be cut with political impunity, for no trade union, no arms manufacturer, no lobby will bring pressure to bear upon Congress, on our behalf.

To do our job, we require people and money.

We do not know how much the communist world spends for propaganda and information. USIA has tried to estimate the size of the Soviet propaganda effort worldwide, but has found it impossible to strike a reliable estimate. But a study published by the Internal Security Subcommittee of the Senate Committee on the Judiciary in 1960 estimated, and I quote: "The various forms of communist propaganda throughout the world involve a personnel of about 500,000 and an annual expenditure of approximately $2,000,000,000."

I quote further: "It can be said that Moscow (with slight aid from Peking) spends $2 a year per free man to be subjugated. To grasp the magnitude of this figure expressing the scope of the political war Moscow wages against us, we should remark that an American Senate Committee has estimated the sums allocated by the United States to world propaganda at one and a quarter cents per person per year. If the budgets of all other free countries are added the total hardly comes to two cents. On this point the Soviet effort is roughly 100 times as great as that of all the rest of the world." That is the end of quotation.

Yesterday we received the verdict on the U.S. Information Agency from the House of Representatives. We had asked for a total appropriation for Fiscal 1964 of $157.9 million. We were given $142.7 million, that is to say $15 million less than we had requested.

The House Appropriations Committee report stated, "No additional positions have been allowed except for the Voice of America." That means a personnel ceiling—a freeze.

We were allowed $110,000 to cover all representation and contact work by our officers in 239 posts in 104 countries. That breaks down to $75 per man per year. Not infrequently some of that money is used to entertain visiting Congressmen who later deny requests for money for entertainment. For the Agency's use in Washington, we are allowed $500 a year to entertain foreign cabinet ministers, prominent journalists and the heads of visiting delegations.

Another figure may help to illustrate the point. The Russians attempt to jam the broadcasts of the free world. Were we to maintain and operate a jamming system equivalent to theirs, it would cost us $150,000,000 a year. The budget for the Voice of America is $23 million.

Let me share with you what we may have to face eliminating. Latin America and Africa are our two principal areas of concern.

In Latin America we asked for $10,747,000 to cover our operations in 23 countries. The United States, in concert with the other American republics, seeks in Latin America a social revolution across the span of an entire continent within the time of a few years without resort to violence. In all the noble deeds of man best chronicled by history there are no examples of success on so comparable a scale.

The modest commitment of our Agency's resources to this effort may have to be pared. We had plans for more films to show the failures of communism, to relate the Castro experience as part of a worldwide pattern of failure.

We planned films in addition to those already done to illuminate the concept of the Alliance of Progress, films that would emphasize the self-help of Latins and the need for participation not just by governments alone but by people as well. But we shall probably not have enough dollars to tell the story to the extent we consider adequate and necessary.

We had plans to open branch posts this year. We have opened nine in the past two years. Their purpose is to move more of our operations to the people outside the capital cities, to tell our story to the people in the lonely bayous as well as those on the crowded beaches. This we may have to defer.

We have pioneered a new concept of reaching critically important groups; labor information officers and student affairs specialists. They live with workers and students, learning their thoughts and their problems, and then trying to relate what is good in America to what is needed in these countries. They have established contact, they have gained the confidence of these people, and now they need the material to support their efforts: new books, new printed matter, new films, new television, new ideas. Supplying them the back-up they need is now in question.

Or take Africa. We are staffing today 56 posts in 33 countries. Five years ago we were in only 16 countries.

Our role in Africa is complicated by the "nationhood explosion," by great distances, infinite variety, and the constant challenge of climate and culture. We have the burden of explaining America's race problem to an African continent acutely aware that our Negro citizens are of African origin. We are pressed to explain that we are not racist, that quite to the contrary the government and majority of this country support the Negro movement to progress. But we must explain as well the difficulties of moving fast, the limits of the law in a land that respects law. The phenomenon of social change has to be explored in considerable depth by all the means at our disposal.

There is considerable belief that we are a country of extreme conservatism, that we cannot accommodate to social change, that we have no consideration for the development of the rest of the world, that we have never grown beyond what is essentially a 19th century society.

The increase we had requested in Africa was only $1.8 million. What had we planned to do with it?

We must reach the African, setting forth U.S. policy in terms the African can understand and appreciate. We had hoped to set up a regional printing center to produce material covering African-U.S. exchanges of people, AID economic assistance programs, setting forth aspects of U.S. history and institutions relevant to Africa, pointing out common elements of our heritage.

We had hopes of a series of documentary films on how the United States is aiding Africa in the formidable task of educating a continent of people who see education as their springboard into the 20th Century. We would have filmed AID construction for the University and colleges in Ethiopia, or the vocational training school in Guinea. Or films on the Food for Peace Program where the United States has averted famine and provided jobs. This, too, is an aspect of the United States concern worth telling to the Africans.

We wanted as well to open information centers in five new areas of Africa. What the magic of space is to this country, the magic of education is to Africa. We want to reach the moon; they want to reach their own minds. These new centers would have provided books and libraries and equipment to tell the story of the United States to Africa's leaders of tomorrow being trained today. Two of these would have been in Nigeria where the U.S. investment of interests is great and two others would have been in the Congo, a country still living in the shadow of its own crisis.

Or take the Far East. Our Agency there is deeply involved in the psychological struggle that will determine Asia's future for good or ill. We have committed ourselves and our energies to assist people to understand the alternatives and to make the decisions that will point to freedom. Further, there is a shooting war in Vietnam where our country has committed high stakes of national interest.

USIA is literally in the front lines there. We have mobile information teams, accompanied by a doctor, which circulate the countryside visiting villages, gathering the leaders and assembling the people, discussing and treating their needs, both medical and psychological, seeking to tie the country together and rousing interest in their own self-betterment. We are in the strategic hamlets with newspapers, pamphlets, films and radios, with guidance and instruction and advice for a sorely tried people. We use helicopters for access, not buying them ourselves but going piggyback in those of other agencies whenever the need is great enough.

In Hong Kong we have a Center gathering information from the Chinese communist mainland and disseminating that information for worldwide use. From there we feed material back for the Voice of America to broadcast to the mainland; we feed material for our wireless file to convey to the 104 countries of USIA operation around the world; we produce Chinese language radio programs for placement in South Asia and run a Chinese book translation program for one of the key political audiences in Southeast Asia, the millions of overseas Chinese who live in other countries of the area.

Or regard some of the particular media we use. Television grows enormously. Last year close to two new television transmitters came on the air somewhere in the world every single day—Saturdays and Sundays included. The appetite of overseas transmitters for product is voracious. They make us no charge for the time. They get no repayment for carrying out programs. To gain similar access to such a burgeoning communications instrument, the Russians would be willing to pay—I wonder how many millions? USIA gets the airtime free. But we may not be able to make our best efforts to use it.

Our Television Service last year spent $3.9 million. To meet the expansion of world TV, we asked to add $3 million more, and to add new personnel to meet the new demand. But instead we received an unsympathetic response and a personnel ceiling for the Agency at its present level.

This means that two new studio facilities being constructed to replace our primitive facilities would not be staffed properly. Additional production over 1963 would be curtailed.

A regional TV production center in Mexico City would be out.

The most popular TV series this Agency has ever done, "Let's Learn English" and "Let's Speak English," would be cut to one-half its planned production.

Our ability to do timely and high quality videotaped and filmed programs on major issues and themes—such as the President's two recent speeches on peace and integration—would be reduced by three-fourths.

Acquisitions from commercial networks and cooperative programs with private and educational producers would be at less than one-third that proposed for 1964.

Successful current programs would have to continue at the current level, despite requests that would permit an increase of both quality and quantity; Japanese television, for example, has requested that our "Washington Report" be produced every week instead of the present every two week schedule. They will probably have to be refused.

Additional programs for Africa, the Near East, and East Europe, where output is now low, would likely not come to fruition.

Or take our Press Service. Our Arabic magazine for the Middle East, Al Hayat, could not go to production every month as we had proposed; it may have to stay a bi-monthly. Or consider America Illustrated, our Russian and Polish language magazine. Russians have been seen in block-long lines at kiosks to buy the magazine in the dead of winter. The Russians tightly control the number of copies they permit us to sell, but our agreement with them may permit us nearly to double our print run. The increases we requested would have covered the cost of doing this.

This Agency has spearheaded the intelligent use of the motion picture in the national interest to a degree unprecedented in the United States with the possible exception of World War II. This development has taken place in the course of the last year. Its success is evidenced by the response from overseas as well as by the favorable appraisal of the effort by the press, officials in government, and by members of the Congress.

Now that USIA has put the government in the position of having the operating potential to make use of American filmmaking resources, it is indeed a setback to receive a vote of no confidence from the House of Representatives. On last year's limited production budget, we produced examples of what might be done in various fields with motion pictures. In Fiscal Year 1964 we had expected to have funds available to put America's most talented filmmakers to work on themes of priority importance. The necessary funds included an increase in per picture costs and an increase in the number of pictures.

We intended to treat such issues as America's racial challenge in a series of films which would explain to the world this most basic of American problems. We wanted to do 30 films on subjects such as Disarmament and the need for a Test Ban, Progress through Freedom on the U.S. social scene, and the results of communism. The budget cuts may slice this plan in half.

Of great significance is our book program—significant because, in a world awakening to the revolution of education, books and the access to knowledge will guide the minds of those new literates who will dream great dreams. The communists are aware of this. Last year they published 40,000,000 volumes in non-bloc languages. They caused to be published around the world another 100 million. USIA last year published five million. This year we asked for funds to publish some three million more, particularly in the Spanish and Portuguese for Latin America where we have managed to build a modest momentum. The House appropriation could hold us at our present level. And our modest goal was for eight million next year against their 140 million this year.

Of course, all these things I mention—and they are but a partial list—will not have to be eliminated. But all have varying degrees of urgency, and the restrictive judgment of the House of Representatives forces us to painful choices in which some national interest must be compromised and some precious national opportunities cannot be seized.

Most people in this country never know of our Agency unless it gets into trouble. Well, learn of us now, because we're in trouble.

We had asked for a budget increase that we thought we could spend efficiently and effectively. We want only the tools of our trade. We shall try to restore the cuts in the Senate.

Either the House of Representatives believes in the potency of ideas and the importance of information or it does not. And on the record, it does not so believe. It is the function of the Congress to decide these matters. But it is the duty of those concerned with this global struggle, however, to utter warnings as to the consequences that may be expected to flow from a policy which denies the United States the opportunity to compete on equal terms. Money alone won't do it—the propaganda of the deed is more important than the propaganda of the word. But we must be heard and we must be read, particularly by those in the emerging nations who are examining old ideas and new allegiances. If we fail, history will take its revenge.

The United States Information Agency is not a perfect instrument, but it is maturing and its product is improving. It is the government agency charged with the responsibility of exporting ideas and information. More money will not guarantee success, but insufficient money will threaten failure.

We are being out-spent, out-published, and out-broadcast. We are a first-class power. We require a first-class voice abroad.

9. National Education Association, July 1, 1963

Human history becomes more and more a race between education and catastrophe... Yet, clumsily or smoothly, the world, it seems, progresses and will progress.
H.G. Wells

Edward R. Murrow's entire professional career was tied to the field of education in one way or another. He was dedicated to education of the public through his radio and television broadcasts and benefitted from Ida Mae Lou Anderson's Pygmalion-like devotion to his persuasive speech prowess, a skill he used the rest of his life. Murrow is viewed to this day as the intellectual face of journalism and this may explain why he gave more Agency talks to educational groups like the National Education Association (NEA), the largest educational lobby in the United States.

Murrow's first professional job at age 22 was to serve as a youth leader among leaders as the President of the National Student Federation of America (1930-1932). Founded at Princeton University in 1925, the Federation represented the interests of students and student government leaders across America. Specifically, NSFA's purpose was to "achieve a spirit of unity among students of the United States; to give consideration to questions affecting student interests; develop an intelligent student opinion on questions of national importance; and foster understanding among students of the world in furtherance of enduring world peace."[131] The organization lasted until the time of America's entry into World War II. He then served as Assistant Director at the Institute of International Education (IIE), founded in 1919, which manages international exchange grants such as the Fulbright Student and Scholar Programs. It was during his IIE tenure that Murrow became involved in the Emergency Committee to Aid Displaced German Scholars, which brought scholars and professors under threat from Hitler to the United States. His first job with the Columbia Broadcasting System was to serve as Director of Talks and Education (1935-1937).

At the time of his appointment to USIA in 1961, Murrow had received twelve honorary degrees and was a lifetime member of the Board of Trustees, Institute of International Education and the Council on Foreign Relations. If he hadn't fallen into the broadcasting field, he might have well become an Ivy League professor.

In the following speech before NEA, Murrow calls on educators to see their roles as peacemakers whose "weapons are ideas; our battleground the human mind." Education is primary to USIA's mission, he says, since, like the best educators, the agency aims to enlighten as much as educate about American foreign policy.

The race for the allegiance of minds is a fierce one. The Soviets mirror the United States in rhetoric: they say they stand for peace, food, the future, and for children, but use such words as a smokescreen to undermine freedom and human dignity.

Murrow takes an opportunity to express his "grave disappointment" with the House of Representatives in Congress, which has cut his budget just when there is evidence of its effectiveness by the barrage of publicity from the Central Committee. On a budget one-third the size of the annual budget of the University of California and just a little more than the amount spent annually by the city school system in Detroit, Murrow must work to "tell the truth, because it is right and because we must be believable."

America's ideological enemy, worldwide Communism, doesn't have a narrow path of truth but a broad bandwidth to use whatever methods and means to undermine the American experience and message. Part of that message, according to Murrow, is to continue to report progress in race relations in America.

Murrow, just seven months shy of his resignation from the United States Information Agency, tells the NEA audience that Congress is cheating the official efforts to speak on behalf of the United States Government. "The Congress appropriates the money but we shall all share the consequences." He has clearly not lost his dogmatic delivery style, which had been his stock and trade as a journalist and what he had tried to temper as a government official.

Edward R. Murrow
National Education Association
Cobo Hall
Detroit, Michigan
July 1, 1963

Three weeks ago today, in his historic address at American University, the President said "we have no more urgent task" than the pursuit of peace—the "rational end of rational men." He described this peace as the kind "that makes life on earth worth living—the kind that enables men and nations to grow and to hope and to build a better life for their children. Not merely peace for Americans but peace for all men and women. Not merely peace in our time but peace for all time."

You as educators of America's children, we in USIA as communicators with all the world, are side by side in the vanguard of this great effort. Our weapons are ideas; our battleground the human mind. More than 40 years ago, H.G. Wells prophetically observed that "human history becomes more and more a race between education and catastrophe." Hopefully, that race is only begun; conceivably it is nearing a flaming finish.

So it is that education, in its broadest sense, is a prime concern of the U.S. Information Agency. We seek to further an enlightened American foreign policy by telling others about the kind of men and women who inhabit this country—who we are, what we are, and why we are what we are. We seek to associate this people and this government with the high hopes and lofty aspirations of people everywhere. To do this, we put to hopeful good effect every instrument of modern communication and adult education we can muster.

To share the reading and education bounty of this country in the pursuit of peace is what we seek. I earnestly solicit your cooperation. The need is great, the competition fierce. Insidious ideologies are bidding for the allegiance of minds and hearts mired deep in the misery that afflicts so much of the human race.

Both we and the communists have made similar commentary on man's modern misery. Both we and they use the same words to address the world: peace, food, good health, houses, love, friendship, mothers and children, the future. If our words are the same, where are our differences?

The difference is over our concept of what at base a man may become. The difference is over what our two systems do to human and natural resources. The difference is over the concern each has for the destiny and the dignity of each individual in its society.

Thus it is our adversary who debases dignity, who foreswears freedom, who demeans the dignity of humanity. It is we who have chosen to take our stand on the side of hope, and to proclaim that the only shackles we wear are the limits to which we dare push our dreams.

It has thus come as grave disappointment to me that, at a time when demands are so great and there are needs that cry to be filled, the House of Representatives of the Congress has seen fit to pare the budget request of our Agency.

This vote of indifference comes simultaneously with evidence of great concern in Moscow at the success of USIA. In the past days, both in the ideological plenum of the Soviet Communist Party and in leading Party publications there has been voiced a chorus of consternation at the growing effectiveness of our Agency.

Trud, the official labor organ in Russia, described USIA as, and I quote, "a perfect example of an instrument for poisoning the minds of the people with deceitful propaganda." Unquote. The principal journal of the Central committee, *Kommunist*, charged that USIA, and I quote again, "uses the entire arsenal of the means of mass influence over the minds of men." Unquote. *Komsomolskaya Pravda*, the daily mentor of Russian communist youth, called our officers in Africa, and

I quote again, "specialists in the psychological seasoning and the ideological corruption of the population." Unquote.

In the Soviet Plenum, Party First Secretary Leonid Ilichov contended, and here another quotation, that "Western imperialists have seen the folly of relying on military or economic superiority to subdue the Socialist world and have instead turned to psychological and ideological warfare." Unquote.

We accept that challenge. I came to Washington relishing the prospect of this combat. And given proper support, I am confident of our ultimate success.

There is, indeed, good reason for the Soviets to be concerned. But I must admit to deep dismay that the House of Representatives does not appear to share the urgency of the challenge and our nation's response to it. At a time when we have geared ourselves to a greater effort—both in quality and quantity—to follow up the initial successes we have had, the House has determined to restrain us. Not to recognize an opportunity is a shame—to recognize it but fail to respond in full measure is dangerous.

We asked of the Congress this year $157.9 million. We were given $142.7 million--$15 million less than we needed. The Committee added what amounted to a personnel ceiling for the Agency.

I told the Appropriations Committee when I appeared that we did "not inflate our requests in anticipation of reductions." The Committee was aware that as our Agency operated solely abroad, we have no constituency to complain of injury, no pressure group to press our case, no arms manufacturer to intervene on our behalf, no organized lobby to serve as advocate.

Why is the present sum insufficient? We operate in a dangerous world where crisis is the norm, not the exception. But coping with crisis is by no means our sole function. Reflecting with fidelity what manner of man it is who inhabits this country is our most basic preoccupation. We seek to share the American experience and the American message with others abroad, not in idle hope of emulation but because from such dialogue can and must come compatibility and understanding. The alternative has been described by some as the unthinkable.

I stress the word fidelity because we cannot report an America that does not exist even if we would. USIA is but one of many means for telling of our achievements and our dreams, as well as our inadequacies and our shortcomings. Foreign journalists and visitors, our own film makers and our television networks, our authors and newsmen and tourists, missionaries, businessmen, young Americans studying abroad—all contribute to the view of America from abroad. What we say about the United States can thus be easily compared to the reporting of others. We must tell the truth, because it is right and because we must be believable.

I hardly need insist that our word cannot be better than our deed. It is what we do, far more than what we say, that will determine what other people think about America.

In the months to come, we shall either have real progress to report in the field of race relations in the United States, or we shall be obliged to try to explain failure. We shall be able, in truth, to tell the world that Americans are faithful to our tradition of personal involvement to achieve justice for all—or we shall be obliged to report that a tradition which fathered such great achievement has foundered in unconcern and indifference.

What we say about this aspect of American life in the months to come will depend on what you and other community leaders will do. Our reporting will mirror your response to the personal challenge of making this a land of truly equal opportunity for all.

USIA has been assigned by the President and the Congress a specific and important role in the conduct of American foreign affairs. We are expected to compete with a massive communist campaign of distortion and denigration. We are expected to explain the United States and its policies. A significant part of that task is to communicate something of the American educational process, and thereby to share the fruits of your experience with those similarly engaged abroad. Yet our annual worldwide budget, funding all our activities, is about one-third the annual expenditure of the University of California and barely more than spent each year by the city school system here in Detroit.

We sought a budget increase which we believe we could spend effectively and efficiently. To do our job we need the tools of the trade. We shall seek to restore the cuts in the Senate.

Either the United States Congress believes in the potency of ideas and the worth of information, or it does not. Congress has the duty to determine the measure of expenditure. But it is also the responsibility of those of us charged specifically and personally with the program to warn what may occur as result of shoestring financing. I would be derelict were I not to take notice that the effort to speak for the United States abroad has been short-changed. More money alone will not promise us success, but inadequate money may well threaten failure.

We are a great power and are expected to render great leadership. We cannot expect miracles to flow from the folly of frugality.

I am aware that I depart from tradition in discussing these matters in this forum. The alternative is to try to "make do" with inadequate funds. The Congress appropriates the money but we shall all share the consequences.

In running "the race between education and catastrophe" of which Wells spoke, we must not forget that "the race is to the swift; the battle to the strong." If slowed and weakened by lack of money, this country's worldwide information program cannot maintain the pace required for victory.

I recognize that the U.S. Information Agency is not a perfect instrument but is improving, as the complaints of our competitors confirm. If it is the decision of the Congress that we should continue to be out-spent, out-published and out-broadcast, then that is the way it will be. I do not believe that is the way the American people want it to be.

10. Federal Bar Association, September 26, 1963

I have always thought the actions of men the best interpreters of their thoughts.
    John Locke

By September 1963, Edward R. Murrow had been director of USIA for two and a half years. He had given scores of speeches to American audiences, an unprecedented domestic outreach for a government propagandist. No director, before or since, would do the same. The demand for Murrow to speak directly to the American people, including this professional association of federal lawyers, was unprecedented. He was the most famous member of the Kennedy administration and his star power never faded, despite the debacle of "Harvest of Shame" or his health failings that kept him sidelined from some of the most significant foreign policy events of the New Frontier.

Murrow's motivation to keep talking to his fellow Americans was underscored in a memorandum he first sent President Kennedy in February 1961. In it, Murrow said that USIA programs abroad would better persuade if they were the result of convictions held at home. He was also a big believer in tapping the talent base of the American people, a holdover from the "Murrow Boys" star network he assembled with William Paley and Fred Friendly at CBS. What better way to reinforce American convictions and tap American talent than by public speaking engagements to explain USIA programs and the challenges posed by ongoing domestic strife, notably in American race relations?

Ed Murrow had an audience of "advocates in a cause for a position." Unlike these lawyers, Murrow's jury of peers was world public opinion of the United States, its policies and practices. "We articulate and distribute not advertising for cigarettes and soap suds, but clarifications of government policy and deeds." Here again in this speech, as he had many times before, Murrow talks about global interest in America's difficult race relations.

For years America had been undergoing startling race-based violence that was leading headlines across the world newspapers. By the Kennedy years, television was now in 90 percent of American homes. The vivid pictures of bus burnings and police crackdowns on peaceful protesters singing "We Shall Overcome" predictably horrified the American people. Birmingham was "Bombingham" with a Public Safety Commissioner named "Bull" Connor who fought protesters with German shepherds and fire hoses. A 34-year young Southern black preacher named Martin Luther King, Jr., had just given one of the most inspiring speeches in history to the largest gathering of African Americans ever assembled at the base of the Lincoln Memorial in Washington, D.C. The symbolism of the black preacher pleading his dream scenario at the feet of the white Great Emancipator from a century past was not lost on global public opinion. The world watched and wondered how the United States could advocate for American-style freedom and values abroad when so many of its own people were under siege. The process of how America would overcome its domestic problems would be just as scrutinized as the final result in changed policy.

Murrow made racial violence and America's race relations the centerpiece of this speech that day. No other subject—not John Glenn or Jazz—could take away the hot spotlight on Black and White relations, particularly in the American South. It was less than two weeks after a white man got out of his Chevrolet and placed a bomb beneath the steps of the 16th Street Baptist Church in Birmingham, killing Denise McNair, Addie Mae Collins, Carole Robertson, and Cynthia Wesley. A year and a half earlier, USIA had done the yeoman's job of exploiting the historic global orbit of young John Glenn as an illustration of American technological prowess and sense of discovery. But today it wasn't the white astronaut's historic flight in Friendship 7 on February 20, 1962, that was leading world headlines. What never faded from view in the minds of the two-thirds of the world that was non-white was the mournful gazes of the black mothers and fathers of church-going children and the social justice pleas of black activist James Meredith in Mississippi. America could not officially persuade overseas with its head in the domestic quicksand of Selma, Greensboro, and Montgomery. And how it handled its own "non-white difficulties" would testify to America's commitment to the new nations emerging from Western decolonization. If the world's richest nation couldn't take care of all its citizens, then how truly committed could it be to lending a helping hand to those global citizens mired in poverty and despair?

Murrow recognizes that the United States will have great difficulty in serving its own brand of shared values with the world so long as it cannot get its own house in order. How can a country advocate freedom and liberty abroad when all aren't free at home? He asks the lawyers to put themselves in the shoes of an American citizen serving overseas with USIA. Imagine it is Monday, September 16, 1963, one day after the Birmingham bombing:

> In Tokyo a USIA Cultural Affairs Officer is speaking at the opening day of a Japanese university. He talks of the dynamics of U.S. democracy and stresses that the United States, like Japan, is addressing itself to the solution of mutual problems. The students pour from auditorium to street where newsboys run toward them crying the morning lead: "Birmingham Church Bombing Kills Four Negro Children in America."

While racial violence in America is top news, Murrow also explains the challenges faced by USIA in clarifying America's race relations. The realities are complex, commercial media the world over overemphasize the dramatic and sensational, and the USSR, America's main enemy, takes propaganda advantage of U.S. hypocrisy: this country touting equal opportunity lives in a sea of intolerance. Murrow saw his duty as head of USIA in 1963 to explain American race relations in a holistic context, including sharing with the world the great progress that is being made.

USIA fully documented the August 28, 1963, March on Washington for Jobs and Freedom, even though it took a risk that great tragedy and violence might occur that would have to be equally reported. The gathering of over 200,000 peaceably assembled on the Mall was so successful that USIA's Motion Picture Service unit produced and widely distributed overseas a documentary film in 1964 by James Blue called "The March."[132]

In Philadelphia that fall day, Murrow's voice faltered. A year before during the Cuban Missile Crisis, he had been confined to his sick bed with what doctors diagnosed as pneumonia. He asked Deputy Director Don Wilson to take over the policy reins at Executive Committee meetings. Since that time, his lung cancer had gone undetected and was now taking over that famous baritone that had made him a household name since his citizen of London days. When he returned to Washington, doctors were certain this time. He was in an advanced stage of lung cancer. His left lung was removed within two weeks of this speech on October 6, 1963, after which Murrow quit smoking from that left hand that had carried over sixty cigarettes a day for his entire adult life.

Edward R. Murrow
National Convention of the Federal Bar Association
Sheraton Hotel, Philadelphia, PA, September 26, 1963

Permit me, Mr. Mayor, a brief word of thanks to you and your companion hosts for this honor you pay me. Traditionally in the past when a layman such as myself heard from counsel it was first to tell me what I should not say, and then, in recognition of this sage advice, to advise me what I should pay. I should comment only by observing that I often followed such intrepid invitations to boldness by silence. Today, however, I respond to invitation by counsel with a rejoinder in appreciation. I am grateful for your consideration.

You are lawyers. I today am a propagandist. And therein lies a happy commonality. Words are the stock in trade of us both. We both deal with human aspirations, and with that point at which human aspirations are in conflict. We each seek a meeting of the minds. You speak judiciously for justice; we speak fervently for freedom. But both of us are advocates in a cause for a position. To a degree, we both submit our brief to a jury of our peers, and the decisions they reach are necessarily judgments by which we both must abide.

I feel then that I am not talking to total strangers when I mention something of what the U.S. Information Agency is about.

Our Agency operates in a difficult, not too well defined area. Our function is to explain the policies and practices of this government and this people overseas. We embrace a multitude of disciplines and professions. We employ all the media of communication known to modern man: radio, television, movies, press, book publishing, exhibits and the arts. We are involved in an entire range of problems: a press run in Beirut, an exhibition in Turin, a stage performance in Munich and radio relays in Colombo. From a news telecast in Bogotá to a soundtracked film strip in Paris to a book typeset in Manila—upon all the myriad of details we initiate, we create, we facilitate.

Even more important we must deal amidst the intangibles: the difficult, delicate human art of persuasion. For by word-of-mouth, by cultivated personal contact abroad, we seek to persuade others of the rightness of our view and that our actions and our goals are in harmony with theirs.

We deal not only in communications but also in policy. We articulate and distribute not advertising for cigarettes and soapsuds but clarifications of government policy and deeds. And we speak in many languages to many people of vastly different cultures and styles, of vastly differing levels of comprehension. We must deal also with a very considerable
pre-conditioning foreigners have had to the image and the ideas of America. We must deal with the realities of their fears, their concerns, their stereotypes—however unjustified, their existence is real—of the product we promote: the actions and the hopes of the United States.

We have had occasion to be together in the past, lawyers and my Agency. One of our prouder present projects is called "Law Books, USA," undertaken in cooperation with the Foundation of the Federal Bar Association. This is a project whereby private citizens, just as they would buy a CARE package, may buy a packet of books on the law. USIA posts abroad will then distribute those books to libraries, lawyers, legislators, judges, and students. For $8 one buys these seven books:

"Spirit of Liberty" by Learned Hand.
"The Nature of the Judicial Process," by Benjamin Cardozo.
"Talks on American Law," by Harold J. Berman.
"Brandeis Reader," by Erwin Pollack.
"Equal Justice Under Law," by Carroll Moreland.
"American Constitution Reader," by Robert McKay.
"American Jurisprudence Reader," by Thomas Cowan.

Under a nonprofit scheme, only $8 will put this packet encompassing America's judicial genius into the vortex of intense curiosity overseas as to what our institutions and people are like. Purchases, if sent to the Foundation of the Federal Bar Association (1815 H Street, N.W.) in Washington, D.C., are tax deductible. I earnestly solicit your participation.

Lawyers and USIA have other contact as well. The Conference on World Peace Through Law in Athens this summer past was the subject of attention and coverage in all of our worldwide media. Several participants there—Chief Justice Warren, Judge Thurgood Marshall, and Civil Rights Commission Staff Director Berl Bernhard—followed this with a tour of several countries in Africa. Reports from our posts abroad were impressive in terms of the impact on Africans with whom they spoke.

Marshall capsuled it nicely in responding to a question as to why he had come to Africa. He said they were there on a sort of educational-cultural exchange for the United States, that this country "…had sent Louis Armstrong to toot, Harry Belafonte to sing, and us lawyers to talk."

Mr. Chairman, I am neither a tooter nor a singer. Neither am I a lawyer. And as I am aware that a much talking bureaucrat is like an ill-tuned instrument, I fear I may yet give you occasion to reflect on the propriety of your invitation to me.

Other sources tell me Marshall lived up to his self-professed credentials as a talker in Africa. At a question-and-answer session following a talk to a highly receptive audience, Marshall had been badgered by several incessant communist student questioners. One followed him from the hall, grabbing at his sleeve and arguing in a loud voice, until Marshall finally turned in exasperation: "I've answered your questions. What do you want of me now?" The haughty student said in a loud voice: "Take a message to the Supreme Court. Tell them to take seriously their responsibility in race relations." The irrepressible Marshall, somewhat struck by this, thundered back: "Good. And now take a message to yourself. Tell yourself to go straight to hell."

The student, I am told, appeared at no more sessions.

Race relations, I am told, took up the conversations of these gentlemen to the near exclusion of almost everything else. Mr. Bernhard mentions, for example, that in Ethiopia Chief Justice Warren's sessions with judges and lawyers, his press conferences and public appearances, must have concerned themselves 90% of the time with America's racial problem.

It may surprise you to learn that foreign peoples are so concerned with our domestic difficulty. It is no surprise to those of us who work with foreign affairs. There is no single subject month in and month out that so consistently occupies the cares and curiosities of other peoples about the United States. Putting John Glenn into orbit puts his name in every headline in the world. But James Meredith may be as well known around the world, and that while America's space sensations rise and fall in world attention, America's race relations seem to remain in the undiminished spotlight.

It is not then more bold assertion to state that in the field of civil rights and racial relations our Agency, speaking in behalf of the people of this country, has its greatest difficulty. Events here plague us over there. When the Honorable G.L. Mehta, the former Ambassador of India to the United States, was refused service in a Texas restaurant due to his color, it is no answer to say to Indians that unfortunately the Ambassador was mistaken for a Negro.

An official foreign diplomatic visitor was greeted at the Washington airport on his first trip to the United States. He gave his welcome to his host with eyes fixed firmly on the ground. When asked why he persisted in staring at a spot in front of his feet, the diplomat answered, "I am afraid I shall see a white woman. When a man of color looks at a white woman in America mobs of white people may tear him to pieces."

Or take the African Cabinet Minister who with a full day of appointments in Washington cancelled everything to go to Mississippi for the funeral of the slain civil rights leader Medgar Evers. To him that was the most important place in this country on that day.

Or the African student who deliberately provoked having service refused him in a restaurant due to his color so that he could have a feeling of camaraderie and understand what it is like to be an American Negro.

These, of course, relate to foreigners in our country. The responsibility of my Agency is the obverse of this: lands where we Americans are foreigners and other peoples are the hosts.

At a time not of our choosing we have been cast as custodian of man's right to self determine his freedom. It is not a role we have sought. Having shouldered it, we do not now shirk it.

Its import is that in country after country we have a responsibility of awesome sobriety. With responsibility comes renown. Privacy has become a privilege of the past. Ours is now the fishbowl world where we become the focus of many men's attention and curiosity.

How they see us conduct ourselves may well deeply influence how they choose to conduct themselves in relation to us and our Communist adversary.

My Agency's responsibility is to translate the policies and practices of this government into terms meaningful to the foreigner. But how does one pursue this task when, as occurred with one of our foreign service officers, an explanation to an African official was interrupted by the cutting query: "Why are you trying to kill my people in Mississippi?"

What does one do when the foreign minister of a country opens a meeting with a USIA officer by commenting that he came to America believing in our ideals and heritage of a free land, but lost that belief on confronting the reality of racial discrimination here. He has returned to his country, in his own words, bitterly disillusioned with the United States. How well does one then continue the business of diplomacy or politics with that foreign minister?

Or take the example of an English language teacher in a leftist African country where students week after week carpingly criticize America's racial dilemma. After some nine months the students finally acknowledged the fact of progress as reported by the USIA teacher and commended the United States for it. The next morning headlines carried the name of James Meredith and two men killed in the rioting in Mississippi. That very day the students quietly condemned the teacher: "You lied. We no longer have confidence in you or the United States."

All these examples occurred in Africa. But reactions to race difficulties are not a problem only in Africa. They plague us in Europe, they assault us in Latin America, they bedevil us in the Far East, they in short mock every virtue that we tell others the United States stands for. Wherever men have ears to hear and eyes to see and read they learn that USIA words sometimes fall short of USA deeds.

Put yourself in the following hypothetical circumstances. You are an American citizen serving with USIA abroad. It is Monday morning, September 16, a date recent enough for us to recall the headlines. These are some of the hypothetical things that might have happened to USIA around the world:

In Tokyo a USIA Cultural Affairs Officer is speaking at the opening day of a Japanese university. He talks of the dynamics of U.S. democracy and stresses that the United States, like Japan, is addressing itself to the solution of mutual problems. The students pour from auditorium to street where newsboys run toward them crying the morning lead: "Birmingham Church Bombing Kills Four Negro Children in America."

In Rio de Janeiro a USIA press officer is conferring with a features editor of the Sunday paper. He has brought the Brazilian editor a picture layout on the improved status of minorities in the United States. The editor is interrupted by a copy boy bringing in tear sheets from the wire services with this bulletin lead on top: "Birmingham Church Bombing Kills Four Negro Children in America."

In Cairo a USIA magazine with a Negro on the cover sits on a newsstand. The magazine carries an important story for Egyptian readers on progress of the American Negro. Next to it is a local paper with the black headline: "Birmingham Church Bombing Kills Four Negro Children in America."

In Rangoon is a USIA exhibit set up for the Burmese Bar Association. Its subject: "Man's Vast Future." It has the sub-theme, "We Inherit the Past; We Earn the Future." Burmese lawyers are walking through observing this pictorial evidence of the brotherhood of man and the common aspirations and motivations of our two countries. A Marxist oriented lawyer enters with a pleased expression and holds up a local newspaper headline, "Birmingham Church Bombing Kills Four Negro Children in America."

In Istanbul a USIA radio program placed on local Turkish stations is carrying a panel discussion by three teachers and professors just returned from an exchange visit on which USIA sent them to the United States. They are talking about America's racial progress and democracy in action when suddenly the program is interrupted by an announcer with a news bulletin: "Birmingham Church Bombing Kills Four Negro Children in America."

In Lagos a USIA library, used by hundreds of Nigerian college students daily, has a near full house with students at every table using American books, source material, and periodicals. At a far table one student with a transistor radio quiets his comrades and turns up the volume for the whole room to hear the same bulletin on "Four Negro Children Killed in American Church Bombing."

In Caracas a television station has just finished broadcasting to the Venezuelan capital a USIA TV show on the progressive social institutions of a democracy in action. The news show immediately following opens with a lead announcement on "Four Negro Children Killed in American Church Bombing."

These hypothetical incidents could, in fact, have happened to any of our USIA officers in scores of capitals around the world.

Several morals flow from them. U.S. racial violence is top news the world round. The good name and repute of this country is being blackened and defamed. To all of us, this is distressingly, inescapably true.

I should not, however, leave you with the impression that racial disturbances are deplorable because they make USIA's job abroad difficult. Difficulties, after all, are what we are sent abroad to engage, and in the total sum of how this nation fares the good or ill fortune of my Agency is of but small consequence.

But I believe that these are testing times, and that we are being now measured against the yardstick of the very ideals we ourselves created. It is true that a curious world waits to see if a nation so constituted as we can constitutionally solve the commitment of our Constitution to equal rights for all our citizenry. But the reason we attempt racial progress is not the opinion of peoples overseas. It is at base the conscience of ourselves here at home, the conscience of both the deniers and the denied. We do this because we demand it of ourselves. We do it because it is right. And this is a nation where right has honor.

To the world USIA makes commentary upon where our racial concerns may lead us. Our difficulty is heightened in explaining such matters overseas by three things. There is a genuine misunderstanding of an extremely complex domestic problem with its roots deep in the U.S. past and in the U.S. present of economic, social, and political realities. Second, commercial news media of both this and other countries tend to unbalance circumstances by emphasizing sensational developments. This is the principle that violence makes headlines while nonviolence makes dull reading. Third, deliberate distortion by our enemies exploits an impression of pervasive injustice and intolerance in the United States coming from a nation which claims to champion equality and opportunity.

We are newsmen. As such we report events of racial discrimination and violence as they occur, for our audiences abroad have an understandably keen interest in such matters. But at the same time we attempt to place such occurrences in the context of this nation as a living democracy.

We know that this issue and its problems will be with us for a long time to come. Controversy and disorder will be its backwash. We shall not be able to undo wholly such unfavorable impressions of the United States as this will create.

So our corrective task becomes one of showing that controversy and disorder are inevitable by-products of our national concern over equal rights for all. We do everything possible to offset the effect of distortions and misrepresentations. We seek to dispel ignorance. We aim to supplement oversimplification. We try to remedy incomplete information. Our goal is to obtain sympathetic understanding of interested nations for what we seek to do.

Thus we follow complete candor in recognizing the dimensions and complexity of the problem.

We detail the full and active Administration support of all measures required to solve the problem.

We indicate that the very struggles now compelling worldwide attention to the problem are themselves signs of progress. Democracy in action is never quiet.

We relate constructive movements to solutions at whatever level they occur—national, regional, state, or local. We bear in mind that nationwide more schools, hospitals, theaters, restaurants, labor unions, and housing developments are integrated than are not. Each new instance of integration adds to an already favorable balance.

We seek out and use sources which give a continuing flow of news about significant constructive developments—however unspectacular.

We background each positive item with materials to show that such developments are not unique but part of a mounting national trend.

We focus attention on the support of the majority of Americans for civil rights progress and programs already in operation and in submission by the President to the Congress.

We point out the large white participation and support of the colored man's call for equality.

We underline the positive response of major elements of this nation—church groups, trade unions, business leaders, women's organizations, professional associations, students—and the response of all to the President's call for cooperation.

We look for stories to humanize civil rights advances, telling of those proud but unknown individuals who help to win local gains.

We give prominence in materials to special audiences—labor, women, students—to civil rights activities of their U.S. counterparts.

We explain, as we inevitably must, the peculiar nature of the U.S. Federal system, making it clear that local officials are locally elected and local police are locally directed. They are not, as in many other countries, under control of the national government.

Do not misunderstand the intent of our Agency. We are under injunction to report the rough with the smooth, to relate unfavorable or controversial developments or resistance to the President and his program. But our purposes are to keep the broader national purposes in view—and to report our progress, however attenuated, to the national goals we have set for ourselves. And we shall do this even when other sources of information, however motivated they may be in their reporting, tend to obscure those goals.

Sometimes, of course, this may involve great risk. When 200,000 people converged on Washington on August 28, all the facilities of our many media went into action. Our Press Service cameras photographed its length and breadth, with those photos later making their way to overseas posts for placement in local publications. News summaries on our wireless file, along with official statements and releases, were teletyped to seven geographical world areas. The Voice of America, with newscasts in 36 languages, was on the air with special coverage throughout the day. Our Motion Picture Service has done a documentary centering on the March. Further, newsreel footage went into scores of movie houses for theatergoers, particularly in Africa and Latin America. The Television Service did short sequences for placement worldwide on foreign TV stations.

This has the ring of sound preparation and efficient organization, as indeed it was. Where, you might ask, was the risk? The risk lay in what might have occurred. Had disturbances broken out our cameras and colleagues and copy would have been just as actively reporting tragedy as they did triumph.

From this arises a very fundamental lesson in propaganda. Propaganda is far more what we do than what we say. Propaganda of the deed is far better and a thousand times more lasting than propaganda of the word. Words can supplement or bolster but can never substitute for actions. We will be known far more by what we are than by what we say we are.

The civil rights struggle will indeed be a trying time for a democracy. Our people in a real sense will be on trial. And our concern will be not only with the ends we finally obtain but as well how we reach those ends. The verdict is not the only truth in our national jurisprudence. Democracy is as well concerned with the style of the trial.

There will be other spectators as well in this courtroom of international history. Two thirds of this planet is non-white; they would be less than human if they were not absorbed in the disposition we make of our own non-white difficulties.

They will regard us not only in their role as non-white onlookers but also as bearers of the legacy of poverty. Sensing their own newborn need for a better life, they will sense also the lack or presence of a social conscience in this, the world's richest nation with wealth enough to do whatever its dream commands. If we choose not to make honorable disposition of the Negro complainant in our court of history, they will know that it was not because we were unable. It will be that we chose to do less than honor in the face of injustice.

I am not so naïve as to believe that morality alone will be the palliative for our international ills. Defense is difficult without strength to accompany morality. But neither can the judgments we now seek from other nations be commanded by force alone.

Man has not yet devised the command to hold the head and heart of him who dreams and dares.

Respect and confidence, like love from a woman and loyalty from an ally, must be earned. The American people stand now as a nation closely observed. The jury of peers has not yet been summoned to decision. But when that day arrives, let no man here begrudge the evidence that he himself put into the scales of justice.

The Twentieth Century can be the century of liberty and justice. We inherit the past. But we earn the future. Let us consider our concerns of today with due respect to what we hope that future will bring.

End Notes

Introduction

[1] Edward R. Murrow, Director, U.S. Information Agency, Statement before the Subcommittee on International Organizations and Movements of the Committee on Foreign Affairs, House of Representatives, March 28, 1963.

[2] "Analysis of the Khrushchev Speech of January 6, 1961," U.S. Senate, June 16, 1961.

[3] Alexander Kendrick, Prime Time: The Life of Edward R. Murrow (Boston: Little, Brown & Co.), p. 456. See also remarks by George Stevens, Jr.

[4] Ibid., p. 464.

[5] Murrow at the United States Information Agency (USIA), 1961-1964, available at http://dca.lib.tufts.edu/features/murrow/exhibit/usia.html.

[6] Robert J. Kodosky, Psychological Operations American Style: The Joint United States Public Affairs Office, Vietnam and Beyond, Rowman & Littlefield, 2007.

[7] For a comprehensive history of U.S. involvement in counterterrorism and counterinsurgency, see Michael McClintock's *Instruments of Statecraft: U.S. Guerrilla Warfare, Counterinsurgency, and Counterterrorism, 1940-1990*, New York: Pantheon, 1992.

[8] Philip Hall Coombs, The Fourth Dimension of Foreign Policy: Educational and Cultural Affairs. Published for the Council on Foreign Relations by Harper & Row, 1964.

Chapter 1

[9] Nicholas J. Cull, "Public Diplomacy: Lessons from the Past," CPD Perspectives on Public Diplomacy, Los Angeles: Figueroa Press, 2009, accessible at http://uscpublicdiplomacy.org/publications/perspectives/CPDPerspectivesLessons.pdf.

[10] Jeff Sewald, "David McCullough: A life's recounting in the subject's own words," Pittsburgh Quarterly, spring 2013.

[11] David McCullough, Jr. email to author, September 13, 2010.

[12] Joe Holden, "John P. Cosgrove honored in Pittston," WBRE.com, July 30, 2009.

[13] George Stevens, Jr. email to author, June 28, 2010.

[14] Interview with author, June 2010.

[15] Donald M. Wilson, The First 78 Years, Bloomington, IN, Xlibris Corporation, 2004.

[16] Patricia Keegan and Nancy Snow, "Senator Fulbright: Arkansas' Other Favorite Son," Washington International, Vol. 7, No. 1, Jan-Feb, 1993.

[17] Susan King, "George Stevens Jr. to get honorary Oscar for lifetime achievement," Los Angeles Times, November 28, 2012.

[18] Edward R. Murrow, Director, United States Information Agency, remarks before the American Advertising Federation 59th Convention, Atlanta, Georgia, June 19, 1963.

Chapter 2
[19] "Murrow Made Fame as News Broadcaster," Associated Press, January 28, 1961.
[20] Edward R. Murrow, remarks before the Lincoln Group, Washington, D.C., February 10, 1962.
[21] Press Conference No. 42 of the President of the United States, April 27, 1965. The entire statement reads: "I have just received the sad news of the passing of Edward R. Murrow. It came to me just a little while ago. I believe that all of us feel a deep sense of loss. We who knew him knew that he was a gallant fighter, a man who dedicated his life both as a newsman and as a public official to an unrelenting search for truth. He subscribed to the proposition that free men and free inquiry are inseparable. He built his life on that unbreakable truth. We have all lost a friend."
[22] Edward Bliss Jr., "Edward R. Murrow and Today's News," Television Quarterly, Fall 1970, 71-78.
[23] "Fond Farewells: Walter Cronkite," Brian Williams, Time, December 16, 2009.
[24] This is a reference to a "Murrow isn't God Club" organized by some CBS staffers in response to his demigod status. See A.M Sperber, Murrow: His Life and Times, (New York: Fordham University Press, 1998), pp. 269, 272.

[25] Cronkite returned from covering the Tet Offensive in 1968 and declared the conflict no better than a stalemate, and thus, unwinnable. Aides were alleged to have told Lyndon B. Johnson about Cronkite's conclusions, and his reported response was, "If I've lost Cronkite, I've lost Middle America." There is no documented evidence that Johnson ever uttered those words; however, many in the media continue to report them as influencing in part Johnson's decision not to seek reelection; see Tom Wicker, "Broadcast News: Walter Cronkite's memoir of television journalism from its infancy to the age of the talking haircut," New York Times, January 26, 1997; http://www.nytimes.com/books/97/01/26/reviews/970126.26wickert.html?_r=1.
[26] I sought out Bill Moyers and Ted Koppel for this book because they are by far the two highest quality journalists who exemplify the Murrow liberal tradition in serious journalism. Others like Keith Olbermann, Tim Russert, or Peter Jennings may also draw comparisons to Ed Murrow to varying degrees.
[27] Lifetime achievement awards in the journalist's respective medium such as radio, print, or broadcast or just generally for journalism. Past recipients include Dan Rather (2012), Ted Koppel (2011), Deborah Amos for radio (2010), Judy Woodruff for television (2010), and Helen Thomas for lifetime achievement in journalism. See http://murrowsymposium.wsu.edu/winners/.

[28] Edward R. Murrow Program for International Journalists Kicks Off in Washington, Media Note, U.S. Department of State, available at DChttp://www.state.gov/r/pa/prs/ps/2012/10/199473.htm (accessed June 4, 2013).

[29] The Corporation for Public Broadcasting views the Murrow Award as the industry's most prestigious award, given "to individuals who foster public radio's quality and service and shape its direction." Ironically, Murrow never worked for public radio, only commercial media, but did serve as a public official.

[30] Mark Leibovich, "Edward R. Murrow, Welcome To the Full-Spin Zone," Washington Post, March 27, 2005, D1.

[31] Edward Bliss Jr., In Search of Light: The Broadcasts of Edward R. Murrow 1938-1961, (New York: Alfred A. Knopf, 1967), pp. 114-115.

Chapter 3

[1] Edward R. Murrow, Statement by Edward R. Murrow, Director, U.S. Information Agency before the Subcommittee on International Organizations and Movements of the Committee on Foreign Affairs, House of Representatives, March 28, 1963.

[34] A.M. Sperber, Murrow: His Life and Times (New York: Fordham University Press, 1998), p. 624.

[35] "Moscow Chides Murrow," Associated Press wire story published in New York Times, March 25, 1961.

[36] Howard K. Smith, Events Leading Up To My Death: The Life of a Twentieth Century Reporter (New York: Thomas Dunne, 1996), p. 145.

[37] Lynne Olson, Citizens of London: The Americans Who Stood with Britain in its Darkest, Finest Hour (New York: Random House, 2010), p. 31.

[38] Gerald Nachman, Raised on Radio (Berkeley, University of California Press), p. 406.

[39] Ibid.

[40] Bernard M. Timberg, "Who Speaks for CBS?" Television Quarterly, 33:1, Spring 2002, 25.

[41] "Loss of Murrow Won't Halt CBS Project Here," Birmingham Post-Herald, January 29, 1961.

[42] William L. Stimson, Going to Washington State: A Century of Student Life (Pullman: Washington State University Press, 1989), p. 134.

[43] A.M. Sperber, Murrow: His Life and Times (New York: Fordham University Press, 1998), pp. 29-30.

[44] Though the Committee was officially disbanded in 1945, it produced some impressive offspring, not only in academic chieftains rescued like Hans Morgenthau and Thomas Mann, but since 2002, the Institute of International Education has resurrected its spirit with the Scholar Rescue Fund, available at http://www.scholarrescuefund.org.

[45] "Edward R. Murrow, Broadcaster And Ex-Chief of U.S.I.A., Dies," New York Times, April 28, 1965.

Chapter 4

[46] Cabell Phillips, "Film by Pentagon Depicts U.S. Ideal," New York Times, July 16, 1961.

[47] "The Challenge of Ideas," U.S. Army Pictorial Center, Department of Defense, 1961.

[48] Christopher S. DeRosa, Political Indoctrination in the U.S. Army from World War II to the Vietnam War (Lincoln: University of Nebraska, 2006), p. 188.

[49] Paul D. Haynie, "George Stuart Benson (1898-1991)," Encyclopedia of Arkansas History and Culture, available at http://encyclopediaofarkansas.net/encyclopedia/entry-detail.aspx?entryID=3495 (accessed June 6, 2013).

[50] "The Investigation: Operation Abolition," Time, March 17, 1961.

[51] Bradley S. Greenberg, "Operation Abolition vs. Operation Correction," Audio-Visual Communication Review (11) May-June, 1963, 40-46.

[52] "The Challenge of Ideas" U.S. Army Pictorial Center, Department of Defense, 1961.

[53] A.M. Sperber, Murrow: His Life and Times (New York: Fordham University Press, 1998), p. 693.

Chapter 5

[54] "Murrow's Move to Capital Great Loss to 485 Madison," Jo Sales, Journal-American, January 31, 1961.

[55] Ibid.

[56] "Murrow and the Commentators," Chattanooga Times, January 29, 1961, Record Group 306, "United States Information Agency," National Archives and Records Administration II, College Park, Maryland; hereafter cited parenthetically as RG306, E1069, Folder, "ERM, January 1961," Box 16.

[57] "Murrow to Succeed Allen," Lexington Dispatch, January 30, 1961. Folder "ERM, January 1961," Box 16.

[58] "The Oracular American," Harrisburg News, January 30, 1961.

[59] "Mr. Murrow," Commercial Appeal, January 29, 1961.

[60] "Way Clear for Murrow to Take Over the USIA," New York Post, January 29, 1961.

[61] "The TV Scene: Murrow Leaves at Curious Time," Cecil Smith, Los Angeles Times.

[62] "Three Tough Jobs," New York World-Telegram and The Sun, Monday, January 30, 1961.

[63] "Voice of America," News & Courier, January 30, 1961.

[64] See "The Whole Truth," Atlanta Journal, January 30, 1961; "Murrow: Nothing But the Truth," New York Post, January 30, 1961; and "Murrow Wants USIA Activities Built on 'Rugged Basis of Truth,'" Dana Adams Schmidt, New York Times News Service, January 30, 1961.

[65] "Policy and Propaganda—Murrow's Assignment," James Reston, New York Times, January 29, 1961, E10.

⁶⁶ *Ibid.*

⁶⁷ Donald M. Wilson, The First 78 Years (Bloomington, Xlibris Corporation, 2004), 155.

⁶⁸ *Ibid.*, 156.

Chapter 6

⁶⁹ Kennedy's Special Assistant Arthur W. Schlesinger writes in A Thousand Days that Kennedy had a talent "to attract natural oppositionists—Galbraith, Kaysen, Murrow and others—and put them to work for government." See Arthur M. Schlesinger, Jr., A Thousand Days: John F. Kennedy in the White House (New York: Black Dog & Leventhal Publishers, 2005), p. 239. Illustrated and abridged edition.

⁷⁰ Thomas Sorensen, The Word War (New York: Harper and Row, 1968), p. 123.

⁷¹ Alexander Kendrick, biographer of Murrow, reports that a Harvard classmate of John F. Kennedy, Blair Clark, who worked with Murrow at CBS, first recommended Stanton, especially for his prowess with securing Congressional appropriations for the Agency. He recommended Murrow if the Kennedy administration preferred a man of credibility to tell America's story. See Alexander Kendrick, Prime Time: The Life of Edward R. Murrow (Boston: Little, Brown and Co., 1969), p. 452.

⁷² For the speech in audio and video format, see the John F. Kennedy Presidential Library & Museum link at http://www.jfklibrary.org/AssetViewer/AS08q5oYz0SFUZg9uOi4iw.aspx

⁷³ *Ibid.*

⁷⁴ Radio Television Digital News Association (RTDNA) "Industry Leaders: Edward R. Murrow Speech," available at http://www.rtdna.org/pages/media_items/edward-r.-murrow-speech998.php (accessed August 10, 2010).

⁷⁵ Edward Bernays and Burnet Hershey, eds., The Case for Reappraisal of the U.S. Overseas Information Policies and Programs (New York: Praeger, 1970), p. 9.

⁷⁶ USAID-50 Years of Food for Peace, available at http://foodaid.org/2010/11/16/food-for-peace-50th-anniversary-book/ (downloaded June 6, 2013).

⁷⁷ *Ibid.*

⁷⁸ Edward R. Murrow, Remarks, USIA Honors Ceremony, Washington, D.C., June 9,1961.

⁷⁹ Alexander Kendrick, Prime Time: The Life of Edward R. Murrow (Boston: Little, Brown & Company), 1969, p. 500.

⁸⁰ Sorensen, op. cit., 123.

⁸¹ Morrie Ryskind, "Past Master of Propaganda," Los Angeles Times, February 3, 1961, B4.

⁸² Letters, January and February 1961, John F. Kennedy Papers, Folder Group 2961A, Box No. 184, JFKL.

[83] Ibid.
[84] Ibid.
[85] Ibid.
[86] Ibid.
[87] Ibid.
[88] John F. Kennedy Presidential Library, Columbia Point, Boston, Massachusetts, National Security Files, Departments and Agencies (USIA), White House General Correspondence.
[89] Statement by Edward R. Murrow, Nominee to be Director, United States Information Agency, before the Committee on Foreign Relations, United States Senate, March, J. William Fulbright, Chair, March 14, 1961.
[90] Edward R. Murrow, remarks before the Subcommittee of the Committee on Appropriations, U.S. House of Representatives, March 27, 1961.
[91] The U.S. Advisory Commission members in 1961 were chairman Mark A. May, director of Yale University's Institute of Human Relations; Erwin D. Canham, editor of the Christian Science Monitor; Lewis W. Douglas, former ambassador to Great Britain; Sigurd S. Larmon, board chairman of Young & Rubicam; and Philip D. Reed, former board chairman of General Electric.
[92] The U.S.-founded Institute for Propaganda Analysis defined propaganda as "the expression of opinion or action ...deliberately designed to influence opinions or actions of other individuals or groups to predetermined ends." See Institute for Propaganda Analysis, *Propaganda Analysis* (New York: The Institute, 1938).
[93] Statement by Edward R. Murrow, Nominee to be Director, United States Information Agency, before the Committee on Foreign Relations, United States Senate, March, J. William Fulbright, Chair, March 14, 1961.
[94] Edward R. Murrow, remarks from speech before the Subcommittee on International Organizations and Movements, White House Committee on Foreign Affairs headed by Dante Fascell, Washington, DC, March 1963.
[95] Edward R. Murrow, remarks from speech given to the Radio Television News Directors Association, Washington, D.C., September 30, 1961.
[96] Exchange by Edward R. Murrow, Nominee to be Director, United States Information Agency, and Senator Homer Earl Capehart (R-IN) before the Committee on Foreign Relations, United States Senate, March, J. William Fulbright, Chair, March 14, 1961.

Chapter 7
[97] Jackson, statement before the Committee on Foreign Relations, United States Senate, March 14, 1961, Folder, "Edward R. Murrow, Nomination to be Director, USIA, 1961," National Archives, RG 306, Box 14, E1069.
[98] Norman H. Finkelstein, *With Heroic Truth: The Life of Edward R. Murrow* (New York, Clarion Books, 1997), 152.
[99] "Murrow Regrets Approach to B.B.C." *New York Times*, March 25, 1961.

[100] Patrick Murphy Malin, Executive Director, American Civil Liberties Union, March 23, 1961, Folder, "ERM, Director Correspondence, 1961," National Archives, RG 306, Box 21, E1069.

[101] Edward R. Murrow response to Patrick Murphy Malin. Folder, "ERM, Director Correspondence, 1961," National Archives, RG 306, Box 21, E1069.

[102] Edward R. Murrow, Q&A with USIA Staff Members, March 24, 1961, MR72-96:1, public domain audio, JFK Presidential Library, Columbia Point, Boston, MA.

[103] Edward R. Murrow, Address to Middle-Level Diplomats from the Far East, June 15, 1961, MR72-96:5, public domain audio, JFK Presidential Library, Columbia Point, Boston, MA.

[104] John F. Kennedy, "The President and the Press," American Newspapers Publisher Association, Waldorf-Astoria Hotel, New York, April 27, 1961. John F. Kennedy Presidential Library, Columbia Point, Boston, available at http://www.presidency.ucsb.edu/ws/?pid=8093 (accessed June 10, 2013).

Chapter 8

[105] Nicholas Lemann, "The Murrow Doctrine: Why the Life and the Times of the Broadcast Journalist Still Matter," The New Yorker, January 23, 2006.

[106] Thomas C. Sorensen, The Word War: The Story of American Propaganda, (New York, Harper & Row), 1968, p. 208.

[107] Edward R. Murrow, National Education Association, Detroit, Michigan, July 1, 1963.

[108] Jean White, "Luster Rubbed Off on USIA," Washington Post, March 15, 1964.

[109] Sorensen, Ibid., p. 218.

Part 2, The Speeches of Edward R. Murrow

[110] David Halberstam, The Powers That Be (Champaign, IL: University of Illinois Press, 2000), 156.

[111] David Halberstam, "Murrow Seeking Anonymity in Job," Special to The New York Times, May 21, 1961, 70.

[112] On the Media transcript, "50th Anniversary of Wasteland Speech," Friday, May 6, 2011. Available at http://www.onthemedia.org/2011/may/06/50th-anniversary-of-wasteland-speech/transcript/ (accessed June 9, 2013)

[113] Drew Pearson, "Untouchables Labeled Top Violent TV," Palm Beach Post, July 16, 1961.

[114] Edward R. Murrow, "A Report on Senator Joseph R. McCarthy," See it Now, CBS-TV, March 9, 1954.

[115] Brian Stelter, "'Wires and Lights in a Box,' 50 Years Later," New York Times, October 15, 2008.

[116] Marvin Wald, "Shootout at the Beverly Hills Corral: Edward R. Murrow Versus Hollywood," Journal of Popular Film and Television 19 (Fall 1991): 138-140.

[117] Joseph E. Persico, *Edward R. Murrow: An American Original* (New York: Dell Publishing, 1988), 431.

[118] Edward R. Murrow, *See It Now*, Tuesday, March 9, 1954.

[119] "Film Exports Decried," *New York Times*, November 6, 1961, 49.

[120] Murray Schumach, "Hollywood Error: Inaccurate, Inadequate Murrow Talk Baffles Motion Picture Leaders," *New York Times*, November 12, 1961, X7.

[121] Bosley Crowther, "Showing the Flag: Mr. Murrow's Request for a 'Healthy Image' in Films is Routine," *New York Times*, December 10, 1961, X5.

[122] Wald, 139.

[123] http://www.lincolngroup.org

[124] David S. Cloud and Jeff Gerth, "Muslim Scholars Were Paid to Aid U.S. Propaganda," New York Times, January 2, 2006.

[125] National Public Radio, "The 1951 Introduction to 'This I Believe' by Edward R. Murrow," April 4, 2005. A new NPR series by that name ran for four years from April 2005 to April 2009. Its archive is accessible at http://www.thisibelieve.org.

[126] Milton Friedman, Capitalism and Freedom, Chicago, University of Chicago Press, 1962), introduction.

[127] Wilson P. Dizard Jr., Inventing Public Diplomacy: The Story of the U.S. Information Agency, Boulder, CO: Lynne Rienner Publishers, 2004, pp. 92-93.

[128] Walter Joyce, The Propaganda Gap (New York: Harper & Row, 1963), pp. 58-59.

[129] Interview with author, McLean, Virginia, June 29, 2010.

[130] Michael J. Waller, The Public Diplomacy Reader (Washington: The Institute of World Politics Press, 2007), pp. 26-27. See original Congressional report, "Ideological Operations and Foreign Policy, Report No. 2 on Winning the Cold War: The U.S. Ideological Offensive," by the Subcommittee on International Organizations and Movements of the Committee on Foreign Affairs, U.S. House of Representatives, April 27, 1964, pp. 6-7. Representative Dante Fascell, Chairman.

[131] National Student Federation archives, Special Collections, University of Maryland Libraries.

[132] "The March" was not shown domestically in the United States in 1964 due to the 1948 Smith-Mundt Act that prohibits domestic distribution of program material of the United States Information Agency. The U.S. Congress amended Smith-Mundt in 1990 to allow domestic distribution of such films 12 years after their initial release.

Nancy Snow is an international expert on public diplomacy and propaganda studies. She co-edited the Routledge Handbook of Public Diplomacy with leading propaganda scholar Philip M. Taylor. She is Professor of Communications at California State University, Fullerton where she teaches American media history and philosophy, persuasive writing, and global communications. Snow holds several adjunct professor positions, including at the University of Southern California Annenberg School for Communication and Journalism where she was the principal faculty involved in the establishment of the Center on Public Diplomacy. She also teaches public diplomacy and marketing foreign policy as a senior adjunct faculty affiliated with the Interdisciplinary (IDC) Center Lauder School of Government, Diplomacy and Strategy in Herzliya, Israel.

She is the author/co-editor of multiple books, including Persuader-in-Chief, Citizen Arianna, Information War, Propaganda, Inc. and the forthcoming Propaganda and American Democracy. Snow is a former Presidential Management Fellow (PMF) in the Clinton administration where she served at both the United States Information Agency and U.S. Department of State.

Snow has held multiple visiting professor appointments in her specialty fields, including teaching in Syracuse University's Newhouse and Maxwell Schools dual degree masters program in public diplomacy; Tsinghua University's School of Journalism and Communication in Beijing, China; and the Institute of American and Canadian Studies at Sophia University in Tokyo. Snow is a two-time recipient of a Fulbright Award (Germany, Japan) and a U.S. Speaker and Specialist in Public Diplomacy for the U.S. Department of State and U.S. Embassy in Tokyo. In 2012 she was named a Social Science Research Council Abe Fellow to complete a dual language book on Japanese public diplomacy since 3/11.

Miniver Press publishes lively and informative non-fiction books in digital and print formats. For more information, see http://www.miniverpress.com

www.ingramcontent.com/pod-product-compliance
Lightning Source LLC
Chambersburg PA
CBHW061637040426
42446CB00010B/1464